Advance Praise for *Enchanted* . . .

"Holly Jorgensen's *Enchanted* made me wonder if the little lake outside her door is Walden Pond. If Thoreau were with us today, he would live, love, and laugh like Holly. This is an important personal reflection on one person's quest to live in harmony with the earth, and loving every minute of it."

> – Don Shelby, Peabody and Emmy award-winning journalist and environmentalist

"Holly has a remarkably graceful way of moving from straightforward description of her unique life into thoughtful reflections on society, spirituality, the environment, and the profound blessings of living in and with nature. If this treasure of a book inspires you to make just one small change in your life, hurray for you and hurray for the planet!"

> – Marti Erickson, Ph.D., developmental psychologist, international speaker, and owner/host of Mom Enough® website and podcast (momenough.com)

"*Enchanted* brings alive the rewards of frugality. The frugal life is anything but stingy. The frugal strive to marry their values with finances, and live a more environmentally conscious lifestyle. They know greater freedom of choice comes with a low overhead. By describing her journey into sustainability, Holly Jorgensen is an encouraging guide to devise your own path into frugality."

> – Chris Farrell, senior economics contributor at Marketplace, journalist, and author of *Unretirement: How Baby Boomers are Changing the Way We Think About Work, Community, and the Good Life*

"I loved reading *Enchanted*. Holly writes about vital matters with passion, extraordinary grace, and a clear, individual voice. This is a real contribution to community and consciousness."

> – Gary Gilson, Emmy award-winning television journalist

"*Enchanted* is wonderful storytelling that is also compelling. It leaves me in laughter and tears. Holly has an affinity for communicating with living things that most of us don't possess, and her accounts of this life are endearing and tender."

> – Doug Wallace, Ph.D., former director of Center for Ethics, Responsibilities, and Values at College of St. Catherine, former director and forever supporter and mentor at U of MN YMCA

To Nancy-

Stay

Enchanted !

So glad we met!

Holly Jorgensen

Enchanted

Reflections from a Joyfully Green and Frugally Rich Life

Holly Jorgensen

Northern
Holly
Creations,
LLC

ISBN: 978-1-7327449-0-5

Library of Congress Control Number: 2018913170

Design by Paul Nylander | illustrada design

Printed in the United States by
Bookmobile, 5120 Cedar Lake Road, Minneapolis, MN 55416

Northern
Holly
Creations,
LLC

www.HollyOnTheLake.com
Minneapolis, Minnesota

For Mom and Dad
And
Mother Nature

Contents

Introduction

The group of seven teens who came to help me pull buckthorn said they felt like they were at Snow White's cottage in the enchanted forest. But no, I didn't grow up dreaming of being a princess in a castle with a handsome prince. I dreamed of being Jane in the jungle with Tarzan. As I got a little older, it was Jane Goodall who inspired me. I still haven't made it to the jungles of Africa, but I've been blessed to spend considerable time in the woods, and now live in my own little forest. I'm no Jane, but people say I have extraordinary connections to animals. I certainly feel close to Mother Nature, and I hope the stories that follow will encourage others, young and old, to slow down and explore her magic.

The other part of my life that some find unusual is my passion for being green and frugal, especially by reusing, and often transforming, all kinds of "stuff." You might call it junk. When people hear of my "Magic Dumpster" or how I often seem to "manifest" what I need and find it on the curb, they think I must lead an enchanted life. That kind of enchantment may be harder

The only fairies I was drawn to while growing up were flower fairies. But when I found this broken but still enchanting one in the trash, I had to bring her home. The table, vase, flowers, and candles were also cast-offs, but the lantern cost me a buck at a yard sale.

1

to understand or to express, but it's hardly new. I like the way this guy put it a couple of centuries ago.

> *To live content with small means; to seek elegance rather than luxury, and refinement rather than fashion; . . . to study hard, think quietly, talk gently, act frankly; to listen to stars and birds, to babes and sages, with open heart; to bear all cheerfully, do all bravely, await occasions, hurry never. In a word, to let the spiritual, unbidden and unconscious, grow up through the common. This is to be my symphony.*
>
> ~ *William Henry Channing (1810-1884)*
> *American philosopher, writer, and*
> *Unitarian clergyman*

I didn't always know I was unusual. In July of 2005, my friend Al asked me to speak to his graduate engineering class. I asked, "About what? I'm not an engineer!"

"About your lifestyle. You're one of only two people I know who live the way you do, and I want you to inspire my students to think outside the box." He said they were talking about sustainable communities, and I'd fit right in.

Well, I *had* taught school, and had some public speaking under my belt. But engineering? I did turn an old pigeon coop into a lovely little cabin, solely with found scraps of this and that. I guess that could be called engineering.

But did I have anything to offer these students? Would they

even listen to me, a woman who relished living in the woods, as close to the earth and simply as she could? A woman who was far more fascinated by the lives of the frogs and fawns and wildflowers around her than by technology? Would they care?

Al was right about me and the box. I lived outside the box of American consumption. I'd jumped off the flashing Ferris wheel—the ups and downs and rounds and rounds of sacrificing time to make money to spend on the next big thing. I never made much money as a teacher or part-time librarian, but I lived (and still live) happily below my modest means by relishing used and found objects. I guess I had engineered a free and joyful life for myself by measuring my needs, assessing my strengths, and bridging the gaps with the buttress of my values. So I spoke to the engineers, and they heard.

Since then, I've been speaking to all kinds of groups. I delight in sharing that many, if not most, of my belongings have been free, or nearly so. Whether rescued from the curb, given to me, or bought at a rummage sale or thrift shop, almost everything is secondhand. Sure, I buy new undies, but even those I often find, still in the package but for much less, at the thrift store. I'm typing this on a store-bought laptop, but I've also found good electronics at the recycling center. And because I recycle, compost, and donate, I generate almost no waste.

It's fun to see people in the audience smile as they respond. "I got this classy jacket at a thrift store for only three dollars!" "We grow our own organic vegetables!" "I built a compost bin from scrap wood!"

One woman told me that the two-hour drive she'd made to hear me speak had been amply rewarded by the story of how my parents taught me to save part of everything I earned, and she

I love speaking to all kinds of groups, young and old.

couldn't wait to share that tidbit of wisdom with her children. I'm sure my totally debt-free status gets people's attention, but it's clear that many are also looking for inner keys to enjoying a freer spirit. I was thrilled to have a young woman come back after a year, hug me, and say I had helped her put the brakes on her spending and reach out for something better. I was surprised when a young man told me he was Native American (something not apparent from his nearly shaved head, black-and-white punk clothes, and gold chains) and that my words had inspired him to return to his roots and raise his children with more respect for thrift and the earth. I'm so encouraged to see people open their eyes to the global aspects of consumption and begin to ask where things come from and where they go when we're through with them.

"*Ah!*" they realize, "Concern for the environment fits nicely with my desire to stop living beyond my means. They are two

sides of the same coin — the one I'm keeping in my pocket." While I teach, I also learn, and am challenged to examine my own "greenness" more closely.

Rocking in the old wooden chair on the high, tiny deck I call my "tree house," I feel the gentle breeze of wings on my cheek. A hummingbird, its scalloped tail unfurled, hovers at the feeder, fueling up for the thousand-mile journey he must make to survive the winter. I marvel at his efficient use of a bit of nectar and wish him well on his autumn flight. In sharp contrast to his prudent sipping of the resource is the community of ants in the feeder. They drift in various stages of sugar intoxication, blind to the warning in the dead bodies floating around them. The sweet life, and its irresistible abundance, seduces them until they find themselves drowning in their own endless consumption.

This scene reminds me of the daily news. Nearly 80 percent of all Americans working full time (and nearly 10 percent of those making $100,000 or more) live paycheck to paycheck. Plastic, both minuscule and monstrous, trashes our oceans. Our dependence on oil continues to threaten our security and our environment. Industry poisons our air, water, and food as it strives to fulfill our every desire, even the ones we didn't know we had. So I feel compelled to shine a light on the pseudo-delicious red plastic feeder. But the bulk of the scenes I share are bright escape routes from its sticky syrup.

I don't claim to be an expert on anything except my lifestyle. I have no desire to tell anyone else how to live, but only to offer proof that there are alternatives to following the flock. I hope my humble examples offer strength to resist the barrage of consumer pressures surrounding us. There are many changes we can make and still be, well—normal. Sort of normal. But definitely happy. Very happy.

During Henry David Thoreau's two years at Walden Pond, he immersed himself in nature, hoping to gain a more objective understanding of society through personal introspection, simple living, and self-sufficiency. Shortly after leaving his pondside cabin, Thoreau reacted to slavery by giving an impassioned speech which later became the basis for *Civil Disobedience,* a publication that deeply influenced Mohandas Gandhi, Martin Luther King, Jr., and many others. I felt connected to Thoreau

back in high school, long before I would live in a little cabin on a lake.

My relatively quiet life in the woods cannot shield me from the injustices of our times any more than Thoreau's could shield him. But just as I have found that saving the earth and saving money go together on a personal level, corporations here and abroad are choosing green technologies for economic as well as moral reasons. While I can't help but feel passionate about preserving what I love, I will try hard not to preach. I'm better at just telling my personal stories and encouraging others to find joy by living mindfully. I trust that our mindfulness will lead us

to vote—at the ballot box, but also with our lifestyles, money, words, and actions—for life, liberty, and justice for all creation.

I suspect the real reason some people are interested in my lifestyle is that I'm happy. I don't mean that I'm never sad or hurt or angry, or that I don't sometimes struggle and grieve. I am and I do. But I have an underlying peace that I know will return—a happiness that is not dependent on material things. I am more grateful than I can say for the genes and accidents of fate and gifts of nature that have brought me to this joyful state. But I also believe that we can adopt habits and mind-sets, values and beliefs, that can bring us more serenity than stress, more joy than sadness.

The most powerful of these tools may be the simple act of going outside. One September day I was in a funk, feeling pressured and frustrated by some of life's challenges. Since I'd promised to check on the neighbor's cats, I took a break and paddled my canoe the short distance to their house across the lake. On the way back, I was further saddened by the dragonfly I found, apparently drowned, in the canoe. But lifting it out with my finger, I realized it was still alive, barely. I almost always have my camera, just in case an eagle appears, but today it was my excuse to pause and take pictures as this tiny creature slowly recovered, wiping its colossal eyes while its wings went from drenched to gossamer. When it finally took off into the blue sky, I realized my mood had also revived.

I resumed paddling but was stopped by what appeared to be the last water lily of the summer. The low sun and high winds created a magical scene of dancing light. After taking (way too many) pictures, I had to get back to work, but my heart had gone from embattled to *enchanted*. When I told my friend Susan, she said, "That's the name of your book."

Some writers experiment with extreme green or frugal lifestyles — living off the grid, eating from dumpsters, even not using toilet paper. I'm not *that* green *or* frugal. Still, if it makes us think, it's a good thing, right? At the end of this book you'll find a list of green and frugal practices you might want to try or use in a discussion group.

I hope my story will create conversation and encourage mindfulness. By sharing some of my encounters with Mother Nature and her spiritual gifts, I hope to inspire us all to spend time in her presence. As we rest in her bosom, run with her winds, and drift in her waters, we begin to know her other creatures as kindred spirits. To open our hearts to her touch is to open doors to ourselves, and to know that our survival and hers are one.

1

My Life as a Tree

It was midwinter, a time when long nights and a blanket of snow often turn my thoughts inward. My life was good, but I felt the need to re-set my internal compass. I had just turned thirty-nine, but this wasn't a midlife crisis. It was February 13th, but it wasn't a Valentine I was looking for. Many of my friends were celebrating successes—building marriages, families, great careers, owning lovely houses, and taking exotic trips. Some were even looking happily toward retirement. I had none of that, but I wasn't jealous. On the contrary, I was happy for them and was often invited to share in their experiences. True, I was tired of renting tiny spaces and often thought of how I'd love to have my own home. The idea that it would be more attainable with a husband sometimes snuck in, but I quickly shook that loose. Relationships were complicated enough without letting a house motivate me!

Nor was I longing for an escape to warm weather. That crisp snowy morning seemed more likely to bring what I needed: *focus*—a sharper and narrower view of my future. But I *was* inspired by images from the warmer side of the planet. I'd seen a *National Geographic* special about Australian Aboriginals and the burning of the grasslands. The ritual cleansed the earth of old dead vegetation and provided room and air and nutrients for the new to grow. But they had to light that fire at just the right time, when there were no young animals to be threatened and plenty of groundwater still lay under the parched earth.

I saw myself in that vast plain, needing to clear away all that was not important, productive, or thriving in my life, and this was a good time. For the last year, I had spent my groundwater—time and energy—raising my five-year-old goddaughter. The tender and precocious but troubled child had been my focus as I both led and followed her, bouncing across that rough plain. But now she had left our little home and gone back to Florida. I loved her deeply, so I grieved the loss and worried about her future. But I also realized the groundwater was now available for my own life. There were no young animals in my landscape to be singed by the fire of renewal. As I looked out upon that broad and grassy horizon, I was ready for a new center. I wanted to see what was waiting under the surface that might spring to life if given the chance.

I decided this was the day to break trail, to ask for a clearer vision of my future. I didn't pretend to fully understand the spiritual traditions of Australian Aborigines or the vision quests of Native Americans. I wasn't prepared to go on a walkabout or fast for days and sleep under the icy stars, any more than I was to hike the pilgrimage of the Camino de Santiago, 490 miles from France to Spain, as Christians have done for centuries, looking for wisdom and adventure. But I was inspired by all of these and settled for my own ritual. I would fast—no food, no phone, no TV or radio. I wanted nothing to get in the way of the voice that would come with the answer. I was off to my favorite forest along the Minnesota River, near some sacred

Indian Mounds. I stopped at the majestic old maple where my first boyfriend and I built a tree house. The boyfriend and the tree house were long gone, but the tree was still my friend. It always embraced me in its rough but gentle arms and laughed when I came to it with my problems, which were so small next to this mammoth, just a wink within its centuries. The wise old tree gave me no revelations this cold morning, but surely I'd find guidance somewhere in these special woods.

I continued my trek, full of optimism. But I found my mind much harder to turn off than the radio. Where was the switch for *that*? The more I tried to empty my head, the more thoughts flooded in. I could go back to teaching. That would give me some security and fill my life with children's faces. What could be lovelier than that? *Ah*, being *outside* with kids! I could join that woman who wanted me to help her start a summer camp. How exciting and meaningful; and how fit I'd get! I'd given singing a shot, but did it need a booster shot? Or I could refocus on my songwriting. I loved playing with melodies in my head, finding rhymes and rhythms to fit my stride as I walked through a meadow or the woods. Then again, crafting art was as fun as crafting songs. A friend had just told me how she loved the Indian-style pot I'd made for her, from the clay by this very river. Hospitalized kids had found comfort in Worry Wart, the doe-eyed purple plush character Mom and I had created to listen to their troubles. I'd spoken dozens of times on the 1890 diary I found in the old house, and audiences wanted more. Did I owe it to Susie Moberly to write a book about the life she'd shared so intimately, if unknowingly, with me and so many others?

"Stop! I don't want more ideas, I want *fewer*! I want to *burn* all those grasses. I want to water just *one* plant and see it bear fruit. How can I find success without focus? Just point the way, please, with *one finger*." But the hours took me deeper into the woods, each footstep breaking trail in the fresh, deep snow, yet seeming to go nowhere.

Then I saw it. I'd seen many fallen trees before and was always fascinated with the art created by their upturned roots. The secret sculptures, suddenly exposed by wind, were then washed by rain and time and carefully dressed in bits of moss. But this one—*this one*—took my breath away. The many roots—intricate, delicate, or strong and bold—were perfectly entwined; dancing every which way while coming together into an elegant design. The stones set in their embrace were ordinary, yet each one unique and as precious as any in a finely sculpted brooch, lying on the sparkling velvet bed of snow.

I knelt down and reached out my hand. As my fingers touched the masterpiece before me, I saw in it my life, along with more answers than I'd hoped for. This precious gift opened my soul, and out poured laughter and a joyful epiphany of words: "It doesn't matter, it doesn't matter, it doesn't matter!" A flood of hot tears ran down my cold cheeks onto the snow, melting my self-doubt.

There before me was a portrait of the many directions and precious experiences of my life, and I saw that it was as it should be. I knew that if I'd been truly focused and committed to my music, I'd have been unable to take in and heal my godchild when she needed me. That the many part-time jobs had made room for her and for all the rabbit holes I'd explored. That each of those jobs, and every creative endeavor I'd taken up, had given me new perspective on life and a deeper understanding of humanity. I knew that all my multicolored eggs would never fit in just one basket; that having a potpourri of interests and talents was the gift I'd been given, the way I'd been made. I laughed at myself, knowing that, while true expertise in any one area might elude me, a creative spirit would carry me. That even my failures would nourish me, just as the dying plants in the forest give life to others. I gave thanks for the security I find in my ability to live joyfully on little money, freeing me to follow my heart. It was clear that the things I didn't have weren't important to me — that my definition of success was to wake up every morning and say "Wow! Another day!"

Most of all, I saw that this graceful storm of roots and rocks came to rest in the peaceful, strong, straight trunk of the massive tree. In that moment I knew that whatever direction my life took, whatever rocks I tripped over or embraced, it would all be okay as long as I stayed connected to the core of my being — the heartwood. To that indefinable Good that some call God, others call Source, and others call Spirit. I knew that because of my nature, my future would never appear to me as a long straight highway taking me to a preconceived destination. But I was just as sure of this: As long as I took each step mindfully, with my eyes and heart open, my twisting, misty path would lead up the mountain. It may not be easy, but it would be blessed.

I came home from the woods carrying a peace that stays with me to this day.

A little while later I went back, eager to reconnect with that beautiful sculpture. I greeted my old maple, but continued along the river, more anxious to see my new friend. When I arrived at the point where the winding stream flowed into the river, I looked around, knowing my prize was nearby. Why couldn't I see it? I searched every foot of the quadrant, between trail, river,

Although I love finding upturned roots anywhere, like these on a sun-drenched ocean beach, none are as beautiful or powerful as the ones I saw lying on the snow that February day.

and stream. It *had* to be there. It was much too large to have been carried out, and there was no road, not even tracks. The foot of snow was not enough to cover it, and it would take decades for it to decompose and return to the earth. Nevertheless, to my utter amazement, I couldn't find it.

Had it been a vision? Had these sacred grounds actually given me what I had sought on my quest? I don't know. But whatever it was, it was real, and true — a priceless treasure and everlasting endowment.

What does this have to do with living a joyfully green and frugal life? Everything.

It's about turning off the media and listening to the soul. It's about preserving and visiting the wild places, so that they can speak to us. It's about the freedom that comes with letting go of the need to keep up with the Joneses. It's about the gift of knowing who you are and what's important to you, and the joy of living a life that is in harmony with your values.

17

2
The Magic Dumpster and Other ... Manifestations?

For fourteen years I rented half of a small double bungalow that was old and needed lots of work. But the price and its location near the Minnesota River made me very happy to find it. One of my favorite things to do on a summer's eve was to ride my bike around the neighborhood, creating my own cooling breeze while I explored. My scavenger's eye couldn't help but notice the furniture, clothing, plants, and household items in and around the apartment dumpsters at the end of every month. I began to notice interesting things near one in particular.

I'd collected many music tapes and needed a place to store them. One day, as I rode by that dumpster, I noticed a shelf, just the right size, complete with glass doors. Not fine furniture, but after I added a couple of shelves it was perfect for my needs. I only have a few tapes now, the ones with my original music that I can't let go of, but the shelf is still perfect—for my CDs. Yes, I still have them, and my favorite vinyl records, too!

A week or two after I'd found the shelf, I thought it would be even better if I had a small table to set it on. Within days, one appeared, right by the same dumpster. It had been used as a workbench and was splashed with paints, but a gallon or

Many people say I manifested this house.

19

The shelf that holds my CDs was from the Magic Dumpster, but just about everything else in this picture was rescued as well.

two of elbow grease restored it to the quaint but lovely maple drop-leaf table it had once been.

When my bicyclist nephew heard I was riding at dusk, he wisely suggested I get a light, "But not one for the bike. You'll be safer having one that moves with your body and can be seen from behind." Before I got around to buying one, I stopped by the dumpster and found, right on top of the bags, a pair of running shoes. They looked brand new, were my size, and yes, had lights in the heels.

That's when we started calling it the Magic Dumpster.

I had many jobs between my years as a teacher and those as a librarian. For a while, I worked for a small company that made personalized guided imagery tapes. This was pretty experimental stuff, but it held promise for people with cancer and other chronic conditions. I was the voice on the tape, gently ushering patients, in their mind's eye, toward a special place they had chosen. While helping them to relax and escape their pain, nausea, and fears, I learned a lot about the amazing power our minds possess. We made a very limited number of these kits and sent them around the country, each one uniquely scripted with comforting details of the patient's choosing. Years after that job ended, I rode by the dumpster, glanced in, and was shocked to see one of the kits. *My* voice was in the Magic Dumpster! I picked up the kit, and immediately recognized the name of the patient, and wondered what her fate had been. I hoped the kit had provided her comfort, and I was glad to rescue it, a reminder to use mind over matter in my own life.

Some of the magic must have drifted down the block to a neighboring dumpster. While I was dreaming of buying the house I'd found across the river, with its sea-blue carpeting and rich brunette woodwork, the second dumpster offered up a set of stoneware with brown and blue trim, juice glasses delicately painted with brown and blue butterflies, and a set of silverware with brown handles. True, I had to climb in to get my "new" kitchenware, but I was further blessed by the relative cleanliness of my provider. Washing my new treasures and tucking them away, I was struck by a strange confidence that the house that matched them would also be mine someday.

Eventually, it was. I was a little sad to be leaving the Magic Dumpster behind, but I quickly found that the Curbside Boutique was a more-than-adequate substitute. Though it takes place on only a few weekends a year, those designated community pickup days bring out discarded treasures like morning brings dew.

When my niece Kym was getting her first apartment, she asked me to take her and her mom cruising for junk. Nancy drove so Kym and I could ride shotgun. Within a block or two, I asked Nancy to pull over.

"Why? There's nothing there."

"Just stop," I insisted. I jumped out and ran up to a pile of junk and opened a plain brown cardboard box. I brought it back to the car and showed Kym what was inside: an entire set of brand-new stainless steel cookware, still in the plastic packaging. "Happy housewarming!" They looked at me with open mouths, then asked, "How did you do that?"

Though finding brand-new things on the curb is not as unusual as you might think, it's also common to find very dirty items. Along with having an eye for spotting cool stuff in a mountain of trash, it helps to be able to see the quality beneath the grossness. I hesitated to pick up a cast-iron griddle covered in a thick layer of grease and rust, until I remembered reading that throwing such an item right into a fire would burn it all off. It was a good excuse to enjoy a campfire that night. The pan came out rust free and ready for pancakes.

Another Friday, I was leaving my friend Mary's farm after we'd

shared a great morning riding her horses. I was looking forward to doing another favorite thing on the way home—checking out the Curbside Boutique. I told her I was hoping to find a wood stove for my cabin. Mary is one of the most supportive friends I have, and is also into secondhand treasures, but this time she said, "Holly—you're not going to find a wood stove on the curb."

When I thought about the odds, I knew she was right. I'd never seen one on the curb before. But that didn't stop me from looking. I wasn't too long into my cruise when . . . there it was. Not just any old wood stove, but a beautifully ornate antique one, complete with ashes and firebricks. I cleaned it as well as I could, putting the ashes into a paper bag I had in the car. (A cardinal rule of junking—don't leave a mess on the curb!) I took out the bricks and removed all the parts I could, but it still weighed a ton—well—over a hundred pounds, at least. The hunky guys playing football in the yard helped me get it in the car, while telling me the stove had come with the house and they were tired of looking at it.

I left with a smile and called Mary. "Guess what I found!"

My success at finding what I needed in dumpsters and on curbs began years before Rhonda Byrne's popular book and movie, *The Secret.* As talk about the law of attraction and manifesting what you want grew, even Oprah championed the belief that your thoughts create your reality; that you can get whatever you want by imagining it. The ideas in *The Secret* were ancient ones, repackaged for a modern market, but I hadn't heard of them yet. As one prize after another showed up, did I believe the dumpster was really magic, or that I was manifesting the things I found on the curb? I had no explanation for how these places seemed to read my mind and give me what I wanted. But the Magic Dumpster made great party talk and certainly helped erase any stigma from my growing reputation as a scavenger.

Friends have often said I manifested my house. How else would a single woman on a very small income end up with a wooded lakeside paradise like mine? True, I was showing people pictures of it long before it was even for sale. When I visited Bob, the somewhat eccentric little old man who owned it, I was secretly planning where I'd place my bed and my desk, what colors I'd paint the walls, and how I'd change the dilapidated basement into a rustic haven. I couldn't wait to put my "new" dishes in the cupboards. I don't know why I was so sure that house would be mine. I'd never heard of the law of attraction, so I wasn't intentionally trying to "attract" it. More than being something I *wanted to own,* it felt like this place and I were meant for each other. When it became mine, I felt as much its lover as its owner. Many visitors have said they never saw a place and a person who fit each other so well.

So I understand when people say I've manifested all I have. But—did I think of, or ask for, things that the Magic Dumpster and the Curbside Boutique never gave me? Sure. Have I been disappointed or lost or broken things that were mine to begin with? You bet. Have precious things been taken from me? Yes, and I've been surprised, sad, sorry, and angry. When Bob signed a purchase agreement with someone else for "my" house, did I believe I'd lost it?

Oh, yes. I recall sobbing as I swam past the house, mingling my salty tears with the spring-fed lake I'd fallen in love with. I couldn't understand how this could be happening. When Bob's sale fell through, he'd raised the price, so it was still out of my reach. I actively looked at other houses for months, believing I'd have to settle for second best.

But do I speak of that sad time now? Rarely. I'd rather tell how, on a snowy Martin Luther King, Jr. Day in 1996, some strange force told me to go visit Bob, even though I'd given up on buying his house. He opened the door and said, "I've been thinking about you! Come in!"

He had another offer on the table—literally on his dining room table—but would rather sell to me. The new price was challenging, but just maybe possible. Bob realized he had over-priced it before, and my house hunting had helped me realize how much it was worth. After these months of disappointment, we both knew what we wanted now, and it was within our reach. That night my mother and my realtor, Ann, bless their coura-geous hearts, made the decision for me. They would help me buy the house, knowing it would be a wise investment. The day Bob and I signed the purchase agreement, we both had tears in our eyes.

I told him I'd take care of Oopsie, the blue spruce looking in at us through the patio doors, and Bob said, "I know you will. That's why I sold you the house." Was this magic? Or was it tim-ing and patience, along with experience, luck, and a little love? Surely a bit of each.

Do I dwell on the things I never found in the dumpster? No. Do I feel slighted because the chair I wanted was out of stock at the Curbside Boutique? Of course not. Though I certainly believe I *can* find a treasure, I don't have the kind of expectation that leads to suffering—the dangerous *desire* that the Buddhists warn of, and which I call an *attitude of entitlement*. I tend to remember only the times the magic *was* there. After all, life is full of magic, and much more fun when we focus on what we have than what we don't — replacing the *attitude of entitlement* with the *gratitude of enlightenment.*

I'm always thankful when I find myself in the right place at the right time, and usually whisper "*Thank you!*" to the universe. But is it magic, or intention, or *attention?* We naturally notice things we think about. When you buy a car, you start seeing similar cars on the road. If you're dating a guy with long hair, you notice other guys with long hair. If your grandpa smoked a certain cigar, you are drawn to that sweet smell, even decades later. Police officers are trained to see much more than we do as they cruise a neighborhood. An artist or photographer sees subtleties of light and color that escape most of us. By the same token, growing up on rummage sales trained my eye to pick out treasures. Mountains of motley clothing on long tables in church basements is a much better training ground than rows and rows of similar clothes on neat racks at the mall.

I do write lists, but they are "finding" lists as much as shopping lists. Again and again I have thought of something — a leather jacket, a set of knives, a microwave, a window or door — that I'd like to have, and then found it for free later. But is *thought* the key word, or *later?* I guess because I don't buy things until I'm *positive* I really want them, I often delay. Somehow, once I'm sure of what I want, the item appears for free. It might be just a close-enough approximation, but sometimes my find is even better than I'd hoped. That was the case when I dug into the bottom of a box on the bottom of a pile on the curb, and found a set of eighty-four pieces of flatware, looking brand-new in their own silverware tray. Can you guess what the monogram was? Of course. H for Holly. The only piece missing was a butter knife, and I already had one. Yes, I mean one that matched—the same pattern, with the H.

Sometimes I really wonder how these little miracles happen, but I do know that if I had bought these things instead of waiting and looking through the piles on the curb or at a rummage sale, I'd have spent more money and had less fun. Whatever phenomenon makes this happen, it has taught me about abundance and given me faith that what I need will be provided. Maybe that's why I asked my neighbors if I could try their old TV remote before they recycled it, on the chance that it might work with my old TV. It did.

I'm sure my optimistic nature and willingness to wait, to try, and to look in the oddest of places has a lot to do with my "manifesting." But my belief that I can find something is not a magic tool. It is grounded in my experience. Treasures I've found have created my beliefs at least as much as my beliefs have created the treasures.

I have also learned from experience that life dispenses its share of nasty surprises—tragedies, large or small, that we never saw coming, never imagined, and have trouble believing even when we see them. Whether fabulous or catastrophic, such "surprises" repeatedly belie the theory that our thoughts create our reality. As much as I'd like to accept credit for creating all of my many blessings, I won't, because I'm not willing to blame suffering people, especially children, for creating the disasters that befall them. Though that philosophy may assuage the guilt that often accompanies affluence, it seems both illogical and destructive, and is simply not for me to judge. The cold fact is that many people carry a burden of suffering they never chose and have struggled mightily to avoid.

But in some areas, I am convinced that our thoughts influence not only our reality, but also that of others. In my teaching years I often witnessed something which studies confirm: learners do better when teachers expect them to do well. Lower expectations, whether through the study's design or the prejudices of the teachers, lower the performance (and therefore the learning and the future success) of the students. How much do our own limited expectations of ourselves and others limit the fulfillment, or even the dreaming, of our dreams?

My favorite of the poems I've written is also the shortest. Like so many other gifts, it was given to me by a tree. I was walking in the woods in late winter. As I turned toward a simple branch and saw greening buds hiding under the snow, it came to me:

I am a tree full of snow-covered buds.
Spring comes on the wings of my believing.

At that time in my life I passionately wanted to try singing professionally, but remained full of fear and doubt. After all, I had no experience or training, just a love of music and a burning desire. I had sung just enough to know that when I didn't believe I could sing, I couldn't. Fear would close my lungs, steal my words, and twist my face into embarrassment. Yet I'd also had those "magical" moments when my love for the song somehow transformed paralyzing fright into a happy flight. I may not have given a technically great performance, but believing in the power of music was enough to summon its joy for me and my audience. That freeing experience was an early step as I learned to banish the negative thoughts; to remind myself that no one was forcing me to sing. I *wanted* to do this, had worked hard to do this, and would do as well as my preparation allowed. It was show time. Time to evict the fear and invite the magic.

Were my thoughts—negative or positive—creating my reality? You bet they were. On the other hand, who hasn't seen a talent show contestant who is sure, to the core, that she is on

I am a tree
full of snow-covered buds.
Spring comes
on the wings of my believing.

her way to stardom, when, well, she isn't. Any nurse in a psychiatric ward has seen people who believe things with their whole hearts and souls. They create that reality for themselves, but their reality is not the one that everyone around them sees. Surely a bird has no doubt that it flies freely into the clear blue

sky, yet the bird's belief does not save it from the cruel solidity of glass.

Thoreau wrote, "If one advances confidently in the direction of his dreams, and endeavors to live the life which he has imagined, he will meet with a success unexpected in common hours." That makes sense to me. Imagine it, yes, and be confident. But don't forget to *endeavor.* Even if it means climbing into a dumpster, magic or not.

Some ask why I don't manifest a winning lottery ticket instead of my trashy treasures. Perhaps because I already feel rich. Or maybe my success in "creating" what I want is related to my wanting simple things. Yes, I found and acquired my dream home, but it was a one-bedroom, needing lots of work. Yes, I consider my wild acre a paradise, but mine is a challenging little paradise full of buckthorn, rocks, poison ivy, and ticks. It remains paradise only as long as I am willing and able to keep it up. My friends were astounded when they saw the nice couch I found on the curb. I told them it was perfect and had appeared right after I'd looked at the furniture store to decide what I really wanted. In truth, I'd have preferred brown wicker to the white, but I knew I could paint it if I decided to. The fabric was slightly worn in one spot, but prettier than the one at the store. In other words, it was good enough, so I decided to see it as "perfect" for me. Besides, it was free! (I happily insisted on giving twenty dollars to the sweet older lady who cleaned it before putting it on

Connie Jean looks lovely in a gown from the Curbside Boutique, sitting on my "perfect" couch. Nearly everything around her was also free.

the curb.) Attaining abundance is related to a realistic concept of what is "enough." Mine is a long way from that of many who buy into our culture's insistence on perfection. When I see long lines of people waiting to buy lottery tickets because the pot has grown to a billion, I can't help but wonder if their goal is to have enough, abundance, or *extravagance*. I've never bought a lottery ticket, but I think I could do plenty with a million!

I learned something else about abundance from my neighbor Rich's green beans. When I was doggy-sitting his yellow lab Teddy and watching the garden, I politely left the beans on the vine for Rich's return, only to hear him exclaim, "You didn't pick the beans! If you don't pick them, they won't make more." *Uh oh*. Big life lesson.

When my grandmother died, I found brand-new towels in her drawer while the ones she used were threadbare. She was ninety-three. What was she saving the new ones for? Did she prefer the softness of the gauzy ones, or was it the Lake Wobegon thriftiness in her genes — and in mine? I have often tucked my own things away for later, only to find them musty or dusty or obsolete when "later" came. While a belief in abundance can sometimes lead us into over-consumption, an understanding of it can also guide us to use things, enjoy things, and let things go at the right time.

We Americans certainly should be able to believe in abundance, if anyone can. Yet the rash of hoarding in this country belies rational thinking. Possessions stuff our closets, garages, and basements, growing like weeds until they force some into narrow paths winding through their own homes. Is this a modern phenomenon? In 1854, at his spare and simple cabin at Walden Pond, Thoreau wrote, "Most of the luxuries, and many

Imagine excess possessions flowing as naturally as water and sand from hill to valley.

of the so-called comforts of life are not only not indispensable, but positive hindrances to the elevation of mankind."

One might wonder how complicated life could have been back then, yet he wrote, "Our life is frittered away by detail . . . Simplify, simplify."

We are starting to hear that mantra — but only through constant background noise. The mass media, motivational speakers, and hawkers of all kinds preach that if you believe and act as if you are rich, you will attract everything your heart desires. Clearly, some have had it "work" for them, while throngs of others have followed that road to credit card debt and bankruptcy.

Perhaps we could all benefit by moving our focus from abundance to "enough." While I rejoice at the plenty in my world, I refuse to forget that there are millions for whom even "enough" is something they've yet to see. What if we all, rather than staring at pictures of sports cars and island vacations and brass rings just out of our reach, decided to picture the world's abundance distributed more equally among the world's children? To imagine not only hoarders, but everyone with too much stuff, freed from that burden. To conceive of things flowing as naturally as water and sand from hill to valley, relieving the pressure of too much and the poverty of too little.

Social movements around the world challenge us to imagine more fair and equitable societies. Both history and economists warn that abundance in high places alone cannot save or sustain us. Addressing vast inequalities of income, wealth, and especially opportunity, is not only the compassionate thing to do, but is also necessary to *everyone's* survival. Such a simple concept should not require magic, but perhaps it does start with imagination.

3

Siddhartha's Resume

In the sixties, many of us read Hermann Hesse's *Siddhartha,* the classic novel of Buddhist enlightenment. Though written in 1922 and taking place in India, centuries BC, its timeless mix of romance and spirituality made it a hit as I read it to a tent full of girls on a canoe trip. When Siddhartha, the handsome young prince, begins his journey through both a worldly life and asceticism on his way to enlightenment, he tells his potential employers, "I can think, I can wait, I can fast." Perhaps Scottish author George MacDonald was echoing those thoughts when he famously said, "To have what we want is riches, but to be able to do without is power."

I've often felt that my ability to forgo a lot of material things and thrive on little money—to "fast"—might be my greatest gift, but only recently have I begun to wonder how much the Buddha's words shaped me. How often are we willing to wait— to delay our gratification—rather than depleting our nest egg or running up another debt? How often do we fast—simply go without something—in order to gain something else of more value; like time, space, patience, security, or peace of mind?

Americans are awash in media messages. We are constantly

Dead trees bring in awesome ospreys.

barraged by ads insisting we need a flood of consumer goods, and that we should rush out to buy it today. Better yet, just get online and "click — it's mine!" I don't *feel* as if I'm influenced by ads, and maybe you don't either. But clearly millions are, or companies wouldn't spend billions to keep their images in front of our faces. The frenetic speed of media and "Hurry! Sale ends soon!" messages sure don't encourage us to think before we buy.

Because I don't really enjoy going to stores, when I need or want something, I'm more likely to think, "*Hmmm*, do I really want this? Do I really need this? Do I need it now? Might I find it on the curb or at a rummage sale later? Or maybe the need will vanish if I wait, and I can just do without it." But Siddhartha's mantra applies to more than shopping.

When my dad saw the house and yard I was buying, he said one word came to mind: neglect. I preferred the word potential, but I guess he was right. Because the yard was full of slopes, rocks, poison ivy, and junk, we couldn't even walk around the house. The surrounding buckthorn forest made me feel a bit like Sleeping Beauty, but I doubted a Prince Charming was on his way to slash through the spiky jungle and rescue me. So I began the buckthorn battle and it continues today. Due to the highly invasive nature of these small, alien trees and the gazillions of berries they produce, even the teams of teens who come to help me can't keep up with them.

But above that thorny understory, there was a nice variety of tall trees, both living and dead. As soon as I moved in, a neighbor said she was so glad I was there, since I would cut down all those dead trees. But I *thought* it through, and decided to leave them for the birds. Besides saving myself the work, the standing trees are a magnet for pileated woodpeckers, wood ducks,

An eagle dries her feathers on this dead tree.

osprey, hawks, and bald eagles. (Truth be told, trees without leaves are one of my secrets to getting great pictures of birds.) Now that they are beginning to fall on their own, I'm using the tall straight elms to build things — a lovely arbor and railings so far. The one I was watching — because it seemed likely to land on the house, garage, apple tree, fir tree, railing or deck — fell in the one narrow spot where it hit nothing! I may not always be so lucky, so I do cut some down, but not without thinking about all the critters they've nurtured in their living and dying years.

I have great respect for arborists, but there are also "tree guys" more interested in getting work than in the roles of trees in the natural world. I'm glad I resisted one who wanted to cut down a huge dead oak outside my picture window. I have watched fluffy yellow ducklings, called by their mother, jump twenty feet from the tree's safe haven, bounce and tumble on the grass, and waddle off to the lake. Then there was the mama raccoon

Mama raccoon naps while her kits sleep inside the hollow tree.

who appeared one spring. She chose a stubby branch as a porch and never seemed to mind me watching her. I wondered if she had little ones in the hole yet. Soon I saw the tiny masked cubs, trilling and exploring their magnificent penthouse jungle gym, their delicate paws not yet as skilled as their aerialist mother's. I smiled at every glimpse I got. After two years of babies, then two of just an empty nest, I realized just how hollow and rotten the old oak had become. Did mama raccoon know her home was in danger of falling? I decided to follow her caution and my kind neighbor Mike's advice and protect *my* home by letting him take down the old tree safely. I was sad to see it fall, but now one huge piece serves as a bench by the campfire, another lies at the edge of the woods. Its open heart invites new critters and reminds me of those born and nurtured there, because I resisted the salesmen and waited.

My first year here, my mother kindly offered to loan me her

weed-whip. She was right—the yard was covered in weeds. I thanked her but said I really needed to wait—to see what those weeds were. It wasn't long before my yard was robed in purple and yellow blossoms—wild phlox and woodland sunflowers—and my mom was saying "Wow! What are those?"

I gently teased her with, "Just some of those weeds you wanted to whip."

Now every year seems to bring something new and fabulous. One year the shoreline was stunning in blue lobelia, along with about twenty other species of wildflowers. I have planted some of these natives, like the brilliant red cardinal flower and butterfly-friendly swamp milkweed with fragrant pink flowers, but most are volunteers. Our lake is exceptionally clear and full of wildlife because my neighbors and I all have buffer zones, created by *not* mowing or planting grass down to the lake; created by just *waiting.* That's just one of many ways to be more green with less work!

This lovely strip of color on our shore filters the rain as it runs off the land, ensuring a cleaner lake. It also provides a favorite place for deer to have and hide their fawns. Almost every spring I find a few newborns curled up among the ferns and grasses and jewelweed, moving not a twitch as I take their pictures. My neighbors say the wildlife, like the stray cats and dogs, know they can trust me. That they know I like them—even the pretty little red-bellied snakes. Maybe so. Or maybe they just like the quiet here and that it doesn't smell of chemicals. Whatever the reason, I am blessed with Mother Nature's grandchildren.

As I pull buckthorn every summer, I clear slopes that need ground cover—enough to cost a lot of money and work—unless I'm willing to *think, wait, and fast.* I figured there must be some

Our natural shoreline saves work and shelters fawns every spring.

perennials around a little old abandoned house I saw. Sure enough, there was a bed of lamium. I found out who owned it, got permission, and transplanted it to my yard. It took a couple years to fill in, but now one slope is covered in purple flowers amid a carpet of green and silver leaves. Others are draped in lily of the valley, snow-on-the-mountain, hosta, vinca, sedum, and yellow and white lamium, all rescued from bulldozers or generously shared by friends and nurtured with patience.

When I learned that the Shady Lane trailer park was about

I rescued this lamium from the bulldozer a few years back. Now it blooms on my slope every summer.

to be demolished to make way for a new high-rise, I heard the plants calling to me. I got permission, waited, and, oh, yeah—worked my butt off in the cold April mud, digging up more than 350 plants and shrubs of about thirty varieties. As I uprooted each spirea, iris, or mystery shrub from its home, I whispered, "Don't worry—you're gonna love it at the lake!"

Once the plants were rescued, I couldn't resist going back for a few weathered bricks and pavers and interesting stones before the backhoes struck. Just the right rock can really define a garden or invite your feet to explore. When I walk the woodchip path through my own Shady Lane Ridge, still wild but with less buckthorn and more flowers, I'm grateful to those who planted these beauties around their quaint trailers many years ago, but I also wonder where the human residents ended up. I hope they all got transplanted to places where they thrive.

One summer I found a nicely rustic yard swing made of logs, clearly bound for the landfill. It was lovely, but I didn't really have a flat place to put it, and it seemed a bit too big. Gazing at it as I *thought,* I pictured it as a simple bench instead of a swing. Luckily, I had my tools with me, so I freed the bench from the frame and put it in my car. It sits comfortably on my slope in that lovely lamium bed, needing only a scrap four-by-four to stabilize it. Being close to the ground, it makes me feel grounded when I sit on its mossy seat. The next summer I found another swing, just like the first, but already detached from the frame. So with a little *thinking* and *waiting* (and yes, a little work) I had two lovely rustic benches. One overlooks my north cove, always shady and cool. The other sits on my south slope—the first place to warm in the spring. It has proven to be a perfect place to think and write, and was even the birthplace of a song. Both are now on their way to returning to the earth, but certainly had a longer useful life than if I had not rescued them.

Landscaping, along with planting flowers, often means making paths and steps to walk on. That can be a big job, so I'm not surprised that most people don't think twice about buying a bunch of patio blocks or timbers and getting it done. Then again, you can also *think, wait, and fast.* When a neighbor offered me five big round aggregate stepping stones, I hesitated to take

Five "full moons" grew into thirty-one and this "full moon path."

them, since I wasn't sure what I could do with only five. Then I recalled seeing some just like them at the Curbside Boutique and decided to accept the gift and trust that I'd find more. Sure enough. Little by little, my short path has now grown into a long, gracefully curving "full moon path," and thirty-one and a half stepping stones have avoided the landfill. It also complements my "brick chrysanthemum" — a lovely solution to the puddle in my gravel driveway, created from pavers found here and there over a few years.

For many people, garden design means matching elements, but not for me. One of my favorite creative chores is to build

Brick by found brick, my driveway puddle problem was solved.

steps through my wooded slopes down to the lake. I just love picking the spots, planning the curves, digging in the dirt, and enjoying the result. I prefer natural stone when I can find nice flat ones, but scraps of six-by-six timbers, large old patio blocks, and broken up concrete slabs embellished with moss also do nicely. Not only does this open up areas of my yard that were once virtually inaccessible, each stairway is its own work of art. My favorite is my "quilted steps," made from mismatched patio blocks, weathered paving bricks, timber scraps, and natural rock, all flowing together down to my little dock. Did it take longer than if I'd gone to a store and bought the materials, or hired someone to do it? Perhaps. But all the materials were free,

My mother's quilting taught me that mixing materials can be fun and artistic while saving money.

and a little music or an audio book made the time fly as I got my workout digging and lifting. Naturally, weeds have come up between the steps. But they are graced by the discarded iris I found and planted one fall. I had to wait for spring to see what colors they'd be, but I was not disappointed. Now the weeds and steps are flanked by purple, white, and yellow blooms, adding to the uniqueness of my "quilted steps." I like that.

"Think, wait, and fast." If it was good enough for the Buddha, it's good enough for me. I guess I've added "sweat" to that mantra, but action is as vital as patience in the balance of nature.

4
Shabby Chic and Wabi Sabi

Does instinct lead us to want new, clean, pretty things? Or might it be the endless commercials telling us we should? Either way, it has become a norm to continually replace anything worn or old or dirty. The pressure to compete and the lure of luxury can be irresistible. And if you just love to "shop 'til you drop," you have yet another incentive to toss the old and buy new.

Then how did "shabby" become "chic?" Why would old and worn, cracked and crazed, rusty and dusty become popular? Can "New and Improved!" really bow to "Antique and Unique"?

While we may be drawn to the new and modern, I think something in us longs for the familiar, the comfortable. As we live further and further from nature, in high-rises and office buildings, glued to televisions and computer screens, something deep within us longs for the earth. The crackling paint on an old porch swing might not be the height of beauty, but it can bring us home to the serenity we found on Grandpa's farm. Perhaps a frayed cotton pillow brings us back to the comfort

Most of the things in my yard are wabi sabi — unpainted wood, metal, stone — and I rarely use chemicals. Is that why the critters come, like this snapper who lays her eggs here every summer?

of Aunt Mabel's living room—which was actually *lived in*. Of course, some people simply like the sleek, modern, hi-tech look. Take a walk through Uptown Minneapolis and you'll see what I mean. But to me, the look, feel, and fragrance of worn leather (very different from cracked plastic) recall a time when more things were made with love and made to last, and there was less planned obsolescence. An antique basket releases us from the fear of fingerprints. For some of us, these worn, imperfect textures and patinas carry a bit of rebellion against the stainless-steel sword of commercialism.

I recall when the term "Shabby Chic" came into vogue and friends began saying, "Hey, Holly, you're in!" When I figured out what they were talking about, I had mixed feelings. True, it was gratifying to see that I had long owned things that were now fashionable. And I was pleased to drop into specialty shops and find unusual items that were beautiful to my eyes. But now they were expensive! Whether my personal style was "in" or "out" made little difference to me. I knew that being "in" meant the gears of commerce would likely push it "out" again.

When Martha Stewart started showing us how to spend days and "only" fifty dollars to make something look old, I was drawn to these skills in spite of the underlying contradiction. Though I always preferred real stone, patina, or texture, I'd long ago found that a little skilled faux painting could make a functional piece much more appealing. I wasn't the only one who noticed this. Now that it was officially classy to be rustic, it didn't take long for mass-produced "antiques" to appear on the shelves of big stores, high- and low-end alike.

Along with boatloads of faux-old goods from China arrive boatloads of irony. As we make new "old" things to satisfy our

The stone and log walls in my house make me comfortable, and seem to draw the same out of others.

longing for the past, we consume and befoul the earth. We don't want to wait for Mother Nature to give an object that worn look — the rust, the weathered beauty — so we throw it away and waste more resources, chemicals, and paints bestowing that ancient look on a new object. Eventually, the faux-old surface peels off. Now you have something you throw away because it's no longer "old" enough! Sustainable? I don't think so.

A few years ago I ran across a concept that appealed to me much more deeply than Shabby Chic: *wabi sabi* — the ancient Japanese aesthetic of appreciation for imperfection and authenticity. This earth-centered philosophy has helped me to describe, and therein hone and enhance my lifestyle.

Wabi sabi is about embracing the old, the weathered, the earthy, the simple. It's appreciating the beauty of a single sunlit

Sometimes less is more.

pansy more than a dozen perfect roses. It's admiring the moon the day *before* it's full, or when its full brilliance is tempered by the stark branches of a tree. It's accepting the impermanence of all things, instead of rejoicing in disposables and the illusion of endless newness. It's making things to last, patiently waiting for gold and silver to earn their patinas, for shiny copper to bow to greens and blues, for stone to mother moss. Does the crack in my green stone pin really make it "broken," or just more natural; reminiscent of stones I've admired on mountain paths?

I read in Robyn Griggs Lawrence's books that wabi sabi is Katharine Hepburn instead of Marilyn Monroe, and I smiled. No offense to Marilyn—she has her place, and I'm sure there

Sometimes broken is okay.

was much more to her than met the image-seeking eye. But for me, Katharine was a role model who displayed earthy strength and authenticity, like a tool whose worn wooden handle fits the palm of your hand and attests to the honest work it's done. Wabi sabi is wood and bamboo and stone instead of plastic; rubbed-in natural oil instead of paint. It's cotton and wool and linen instead of polyester. It's natural plants, natural light, natural sound, natural air. Things I've always embraced that bring me peace and joy and *health*.

Wabi sabi can also be healthier for the earth. It means fewer chemicals, more materials that came from and can return to the earth. To me, the integrity of natural materials requests an integrity from us. Sustainability is not always simple. As much as I love the earthy beauty and sensuous feel of granite countertops, knowing the stone took eons to form makes me wonder if we should be mining it as much as we do. I don't know the answer. Likewise, the fact that something was once alive, whether animal or plant, doesn't always get the respect it deserves. I've found more than a few good fur and leather coats in the trash. You might argue that synthetic materials are more humane, and maybe you'd be right. But if we valued leather as the beautiful and precious part of the natural world that it is, rather than a commodity to be tossed away at the whim of "fast fashion" and the quest for perfection, might we be inclined to raise animals with more compassion? When everything we have comes from a store or is ordered online, we can easily lose touch with what it really is and where it really came from. Then we lose sight of its true cost and value.

The simplicity of wabi sabi began as a replacement for the opulence of ancient Japanese tea parties. The hope was to refocus attention on the value of *respectful conversation*, and an appreciation of tea bowls, scrolls, and other objects made more venerable by their *imperfections,* rather than on displays of wealth. As Richard R. Powell says in *Wabi Sabi Simple,* "For most people, wabi sabi begins in the eye, then moves to the I."

In my home and elsewhere, I've seen surroundings that encourage people to relax and open their hearts, to reflect and look a little deeper. Endless quiet corners in ourselves are worthy of exploration, and endless lessons can be learned from letting go of our competitive edge and genuinely listening to others.

True wabi sabi rejects excessive spending on ever-changing fads and a quest for youthfulness in all things. Instead, it connects us with something we seem to be sacrificing to the gods of commerce — respect for age. (Something becoming more important to me every day as I grow older!) If we discard and replace our material possessions so casually, how does that influence our attitudes toward our elders and ourselves? With a deeper wabi sabi acceptance of the impermanence of all things comes an understanding that "in" and "out" of style are no more than ripples in an ever-tumbling river.

Another important part of wabi sabi is *order.* I'm pretty good at that, which lets me keep an ample supply of recycled creative materials on hand without allowing them to burden me with chaos. I love having that doohickey I need close at hand rather than having to run to a store.

But I confess there's one key wabi sabi element I'm still working on — *less instead of more.* Even though I consume far less than the average American, my talent for finding treasures, along with the generosity of my friends (who know they can offer me something used without embarrassment) put me in a bind. I need to get better at accepting less and letting go of more. The fact that I can (almost always) find what I need quickly on my labeled shelves, that I actually (eventually) use the things I have, and that my house is (usually) presentable are proofs that I'm not a hoarder. If friends comment on how much "stuff" I have, I might point out that all of my belongings wouldn't look like much in their houses — which are often two, three, or four times as large as mine. That's true. Yet I'm painfully aware that my abundance of "stuff" consumes not only valuable space in my little home, but also valuable time — my most precious commodity.

Like so many people over sixty, I recently lost my mother

and am dealing with all the belongings I removed from her house. I'm a little compulsive about not tossing out things that can still be used, and I'm trying to disperse things to the best possible places—just as I know Mom would want. Cute things go to her church bazaar; warm things go to the Indian reservation; furniture to Bridging, a local organization that will give it to families in need. Pictures and papers? I'm a writer. I can't throw those away! It's taking longer this way, but it makes me feel better to know it would make Mom and Dad happy. After all, it was they who taught me not to waste and to give to those in need. I'm fortunate they weren't collectors, and that they too had a relatively small house. Still my task feels overwhelming, and is a great incentive to cut down on my own possessions *now*—to enjoy giving things away while creating more wabi sabi simplicity in my life.

It helps to know that part of wabi sabi is "voluntary poverty." This poverty is not a *lack* of anything—except clutter, extravagance, and stress. It is choosing, instead of the quest for riches our culture preaches, an abundance of meaning and the luxury of tranquility. Ironically, choosing this kind of poverty has led me to a debt-free life in which I feel incredibly rich and secure. There is no more recession-proof investment than honing the ability to *think, wait, and fast.* Knowing how to live comfortably on very little, being free from the pressures of our consumer society, reveling in the simple joys of life—therein lies my "golden parachute"; the retirement plan I've been living and loving. If my journey should lead me to more money, my wabi sabi values may become even more important. Without the *need* to be frugal, simplicity can be even more elusive, yet all the more valuable as a refuge.

Perhaps the most precious part of wabi sabi is accepting imperfection. We are all familiar with lives lost to eating disorders and other illnesses of perfectionism. I've heard people speak of a wabi sabi acceptance of your own body, inside and out, healthy or not. So take these two little words and use them where you will. Do you really want to replace that weathered bench, or could you embrace its wabi sabi beauty? Is your nose a little crooked; are your toes a little long? Perhaps thinking of them as wabi sabi makes more sense than expensive and painful plastic surgery. Do we really want a society full of Barbie and Ken dolls, or one where uniqueness, diversity, and reality—not reality TV—are celebrated? Though striving to be all we can might greatly enhance our lives and contributions, we also need a realistic—wabi sabi—view of ourselves. A conscious acceptance of irregularities and imperfections can steel our fragile egos against the arrows of critics, including ourselves. A few steps farther down that wabi sabi road might bring us to a point of aesthetic appreciation of those unique and endearing qualities.

Try applying this acceptance to various areas of your life. I've decided to call myself a wabi sabi singer. Having started singing at the ripe old age of twenty-eight and having almost no training, I never expected perfection. In fact, it took all the courage I could muster to believe I could sing at all. Even as a child, my voice was low, and therefore never seemed to fit in with the other girls when we sang together. I eventually discovered some great altos, then blues, jazz, and gospel styles and singers that seemed to fit my voice. I had an enormous amount of catching up to do before I dared to sing in public. I did so for a while, and I learned much more than the notes. Having gone on to

other creative pursuits, I accept the limits of both my ability and the time I can invest in that art. But that doesn't limit my love of music or the joy that singing brings me. When I ran into a member of a band I once sat in with, he said that I was more "real" than the "flashy" singer—the one they hired. Real—wabi sabi. It may not have gotten me the job, but it's certainly gotten me through life.

I'm grateful for all the advantages that technology has brought to music—the ease of smoothing out a rough performance with digital magic. But I sometimes fear what the ubiquity of polished music has done to our tastes and expectations. When was the last time you sang with friends—blending your unique tones, freeing your inner song, or making up a hilarious tribute, just for fun? Have we lost the ability to sing out our joy and our grief, as imperfect as the song may be? It's the bending of notes, the gravel or stretch in the voice, which some might call imperfect, that gives music what I love most—what blues queen Koko Taylor told me was the ability to touch the place that hurts, then heal it. Live music—long may it live.

Learning to embrace all things humble can help us find harmony.

Learning to see the impermanence in all things can help us to bloom and produce seeds for the future.

Learning to see our immaturity as the moon coming into its fullness may give us patience.

Learning to honor the tarnished parts of ourselves as the patina of age may uncover our true worth.

5

My Up-North Downstairs

In case you think Siddhartha's "think, wait, fast" philosophy only works in the landscape, I'd like to tell you about my basement, which definitely started out shabby, but in no way chic.

I could see why Bob, the previous owner, didn't want to show it to me. Though I was excited by the potential in the fieldstone walls, which were the foundation of the house, they were built in 1925. The rotting mortar was crumbling to the floor. That, combined with dirt, old water softener salt, building scraps, and various unidentifiable materials, amounted to hundreds of pounds of trash to be hauled away. I loved how Bob had raised the house by adding eighteen inches of stud-and-plywood walls above the rock foundation. But they were still unfinished, and what pink insulation hadn't yet fallen away had become condos for colonies of mice. So my cats, Spike and Reno, and I got to work and cleaned it all out. I'm sure they had more fun than I did.

There were studs standing for an interior wall that had never been built. I envisioned finishing that wall and adding another

All the salvaged wood for walls and ceiling were the perfect complement to the stone walls.

After many days of hauling out trash and cleaning, I lived with the very unfinished basement for years.

to divide the basement. Then I could have a laundry/storage room and a sitting room, taking advantage of the patio doors that opened out to the lake. I hung old drapery over the studs as a temporary wall and brought in an old couch. At least then I could sit while I polished the vision of the walls I really wanted there. Friends wondered why I didn't just buy some inexpensive paneling and get the job done. It wasn't just that I preferred finding free materials. Somehow the faux wood just didn't feel quite right for this earthy room. I continued to *think, wait, and fast.*

Then it happened. Some nice neighbors I hardly knew were tearing down and rebuilding their house. Did I want the tongue-and-groove cedar logs for $500? I knew that was a great price, but it was still a lot of money to me. At the time, I was barely making my mortgage on my income as a part-time librarian. Besides, there were many more logs than what I needed for just two walls. I hated to let them go, but I did. It wasn't too long before someone snatched them up—but not all of them. The neighbors called again and said they'd love to have me come and get the remaining pile out of there—just take them!

So I did, gratefully. I hauled load after load home in my station wagon and sorted them into stacks. The scraps were from two to twelve feet in length and ranged in condition from really raggedy to nearly perfect. I'd done the *waiting* and *fasting*, and I was rewarded with the perfect material for walls in my rustic room. But now came much more *thinking* than I'd expected. Just taking inventory of the wood was a huge task. Then I had to plan the walls, the way Mom planned the quilts she made from scraps, taking advantage of the best pieces while minimizing the need to cut new notches for joints. I was relieved when all that preliminary work was done and it was time to actually start building. That work wasn't exactly easy either, but it was another labor of love, moved along by a soundtrack of songs and audio books from the library, not to mention happy memories of my favorite childhood toy—Lincoln Logs.

The result was perfectly imperfect. Stripes of warm cedar tones next to the mosaic of cool stones. The matching cedar door completed the task of hiding the laundry and storage area. Though far from being finished, I now had a room I could proudly share, along with the inspiration to *think, wait,* and *fast* the rest of the room into existence.

When my favorite neighbor, Rich, was about to burn down his old shed, he asked if I wanted any of the very weathered wood. Yes! As I pulled hundreds of four-inch nails from the five-inch boards, I found out why barn wood is so expensive—not only is it becoming rare, but removing it is also labor intensive! Fitting the warped tongues and grooves together was a challenge, but the result was beautiful. The wood topped my stone walls like an honored elder's hair — curled knots and wandering grains, painted in grays and blacks by the patient brush of weather.

One small Sheetrocked wall begged for cover. I found it in a tiny A-frame that had long stood flooded by the rising lake, broken windows staring out like sad eyes remembering more useful days as Rich's writing shack. I had often admired the beautiful watercolor stains on the brown wood as I swam by. Disassembling that bit of history was the perfect cool, wet task for a very hot summer morning. I took my canoe, hammer, and crowbar and salvaged the wood while carefully diving down to clean up the broken glass. I was happy to find, as the wood dried in the sun, that it had not rotted or warped at all, but had

Someone suggested I take a break from pulling nails to document the source of the weathered wood that would grace my walls. I'm glad I did.

merely taken on a uniquely watery beauty. Another day's work and my wall was covered.

I hadn't planned to finish the ceiling—too much work. Besides, I liked the open look, the old wood, and the matrix of green diagonal supports, even though they collected cobwebs. The Douglas-fir joists had an integrity we don't often find in modern buildings.

But one of the problems of being a skilled scavenger is that the call of the doomed becomes irresistible. I heard that a friend's not-that-old old house was about to be demolished. I just had to check it out—to say goodbye, if nothing else. It was January, twenty below zero, with no electricity in the house. Looking up at the three-inch clear pine boards that covered the basement ceiling, I shivered, but I had no choice. I came back in my snowsuit, armed with a cordless drill. I removed hundreds of screws to free the lovely honey-colored boards and give them a new destiny. Again came the tasks of hauling, storing, measuring, counting, then *thinking* about how to make this limited number of boards cover my basement ceiling.

My builder friend Doug convinced me it wouldn't make sense to put in a ceiling without first adding insulation and a vapor barrier. I'd already noticed people were always throwing away good insulation and plastic, so I didn't have any excuse. After much measuring and deliberation, I had the plan, but realized I'd have to use every piece of wood—even the scraps with crescents cut out where light fixtures had been. So I filled those in with metal foil. More music, more audio books, a nail gun borrowed from Doug, and my favorite room had a fitting sky, complete with silvery moons.

As surprisingly as my beautiful ceiling came freely to me, so

Thank goodness for the wood stove that provides heat and heart to my stony grotto.

(Facing Page) The maple table from the Magic Dumpster was the first of many found or gifted pieces furnishing the most rustic room in the house.

did my carpet. I'd been happy with just a large area rug covering the center of the cement floor, but the room was still very cold. When my parents bought new carpet for their living and dining rooms, the installers erred and put half of it in backward. They tore it all out and replaced it and, amazingly, didn't want the "old" back. There it was—brand new, silvery gray, short plush carpet. A perfect addition to the many grays already gracing the stone and barnwood.

Furniture? Avoiding too much is more of a challenge than finding enough, for folks seem always to be giving or throwing furniture away. My sister's attic provided a classic wrought-iron bed. The Magic Dumpster maple table found its home there alongside a Curbside Boutique bistro chair. The curb also provided a lovely futon (needing only a little repair), a coffee table of sturdy wood and marble, plus an antique trunk, perfect to hold firewood.

Of course I couldn't have done any of that work in the winter without some heat. That came only from a little wood stove I'd bought at a yard sale, not realizing how much work it would take to un-rust it. Oh, well. It looked great after the application of ample elbow grease and stove black. A few years later, I was discussing stoves with a library customer and he offered to sell me his $1,100 double-walled stove. It had a bigger firebox than mine, a catalytic burner for more heat and less pollution, and glass windows for viewing the lovely flames. When he asked only $200, delivery included, what could I say but, "Yes! Thank you!"

Thank goodness for that heat, for I had the biggest job of all ahead of me.

My stony Up North Downstairs might be a bit cave-like, but I can always walk out the sliding glass doors to this.

6
Nice Work if You Can Get It

You know the phenomenon—you fix up part of a room and suddenly the other parts start looking tacky. That was a mild word for the condition of my stone walls; the tuck-pointing Bob was supposed to have done before selling me the house was way overdue. The rustic room made everyone feel like they were truly "Up North" by Lake Superior's rocky shore, but wind, water, mice, and even a chipmunk or two were finding their way in through the crumbling, twenty-inch-thick walls. I knew replacing the mortar was a huge job, but it would make the foundation walls stronger, warmer, drier, cleaner, and more beautiful.

I considered hiring a crew of men and got an estimate from them—thousands of dollars. Then I consulted with a woman mason recommended by friends. She asked how long I planned to live there. With my typical optimism, I said another fifty years. "Then you really don't want to hire anyone, since they might do only a surface job. If you want it to last, you'll buy a mason's hammer and tap every stone, listening for it to tell you if it's secure or not. You'll dig out the loose ones and rebuild the wall."

Building in flat stone shelves and bottle logs made the job of tuck-pointing more challenging, but also more fun. The same was true of the salvaged barn wood and pine ceiling.

I hired her for a couple hours and she taught me to tuck-point, saying, a bit surprised, "You like this, don't you!"

I did—though I stretched the job of tuck-pointing the three walls of the sitting room, inside and out, over several years. It was hard work. Section by section, I chipped out and hauled away uncounted pounds of old rotted cement, then hauled in, mixed, and tucked in the new mortar—thirty-five bags, eighty pounds each. It was hard on the hands, the arms, the back. The process created dust and dirt as persistently as I cleaned. But I did—I *liked* the work.

It wasn't exactly "fun," but it was satisfying—real work. Undeniably useful work. There is something so down-to-earth about building with stone and mortar.

And it was art. I'm sure I'd have finished sooner if I'd ignored the character of each rock, but how could I do that? Sometimes I'd uncover a stone deep within the wall and wonder how the builder could have chosen to hide its magnificent face. When I had to recreate a particularly visible edge, I'd walk around the yard looking for just the right rocks. Since all the original stones had come right out of this ground, I knew there were other treasures everywhere. What a prize when I found the right shape and size in a new color or texture! Whenever I'd discover a thin, flat stone, I couldn't resist building a shelf into the wall, since hanging pictures from nails wasn't an easy option. Cleaning the muddy mortar from the faces of hundreds of stones revealed each to be a unique child of the earth. I got to know, intimately, the smooth, waxy feel of some and the somber, smoky black of others; the multicolored speckles of granite; the southwestern oranges and pinks that defied their northern origins; and the accents formed by rusty iron and quartz crystals.

Perhaps someday I'll learn all their names, but for now I just love the mosaic. It's a testimony to the tumbling persistence of ancient glaciers.

The first time my hammer went through the twenty-inch-thick wall to the sunshine outside, the words that fell from my lips were not sunny. The only thing scarier than the amount of work ahead of me was the thought that my house might fall down. But then I remembered how some friends had built a cord-wood house and incorporated bottle logs. Picture two-foot-long logs, stacked as in a woodpile, but mortared together

to make walls. Beautiful. Now picture, instead of the cut end of a log on an inside wall, the bottom end of a wine bottle. On the other end of that bottle is another, a clear one, extending outside just enough to admit the light and make the colored bottle end glow. (The two bottles are first placed neck to neck, then wrapped with aluminum flashing and the handyman's secret weapon—duct tape—before being mortared into the wall.) The result? Jewel-studded walls. At night, a light inside creates a mysterious colored glow outside.

Remembering my friends' unique art, I decided that if I had to rebuild my walls, I'd have some fun and make them truly my own. I went to bars looking for the best empty bottles, creating a yellow "sunrise" in the east and an orange and red "sunset" in the west, as well as a big, romantic "blue moon." I would have finished sooner had I not bothered with the bottle logs, but without the creative rush, I'm sure the task would have *felt* longer.

When I finally finished, my walls had my own glass signature, "gems" among the other "precious" stones. I knew they'd bring a surprise and a smile to all who relaxed in my fireside grotto.

Pleased with my work, but tired, I decided the laundry room walls were "good enough." Since then, heavy rains have periodically caused little floods and called me back to tuck-pointing. For a moment, I remember the work and dread the chore. Then I remind myself that it's a craft, a valuable skill that I learned and want to keep. I recall all the benefits of doing it myself, the first being the thousands of dollars I saved! More exciting is having walls that are my own personal art. Then there's the other benefit—the free workout. Think of the time and money I'd have spent at a health club to gain the same exercise as hauling

This wood keeps me warm, while I split it and in my wood stove.

around, literally, tons of mortar and rocks. And I didn't even need any cute spandex workout clothes.

Did I have pretty painted fingernails? No. I still don't. The hands I remember most were those of an old man my boyfriend and I met on a road trip while in college. I think it was

75

on Michigan's Upper Peninsula; we stopped to ask directions as he worked in his open garage. I don't remember his face, but his huge hands looked like gloves — work gloves, but of finely oiled golden-brown leather. I thought they were so beautiful, and that I'd be proud to have hands that quietly spoke of the honorable work they'd done.

Okay, so not every job I do is as artistic as building stone or log walls. Most people think I'm crazy to shovel my own driveway. If you saw the 100 yards and the turnaround, you'd probably agree. Perhaps I'd feel more daunted if I didn't know my neighbor Bill would come with his bobcat if I asked but, the truth is, I *like* shoveling. I like being outside. I like the rhythm of my body and my breath as the shovel takes bite after bite of the delicious snow. I like feeling my arms, my legs, my back, my lungs getting stronger with every foot of fluff or slush I throw into the air. I like the quiet whoosh or crunchy push, and the fresh smell that says "pristine" even as it stings my nose — things you lose as soon as you turn on a snowblower. Sure, the eighteen-inch, three-day snowfall that Christmas was a bit much, but I did it, and slept like a baby those nights.

If I'd never tried tuck-pointing a basement or shoveling a hundred yards of snow, I wouldn't know I could do it, and like it. I like splitting wood too, especially the kind that splits nicely with that satisfying crack. I'm thankful for the cold that makes the wood split so well, and the warmth the work provides, in my body and in the stove. Unlike shoveling snow, which I can do with my mind wandering where it may, handling an ax requires presence, like riding a horse. I can take my frustrations

(Facing Page) I love the pristine smell of snow as I shovel, even though my driveway is as long as a football field.

out on a good chunk of oak or escape my worries as I narrow my focus to the task at hand.

Shoveling snow and splitting wood provide the workout I miss once the lake freezes me out of swimming. I've come to consider them beneficial, necessary, and pleasant routines. Other chores require more consideration before taking them on. When I found a broken gun cabinet, I stood there a long time deciding whether I wanted to turn it into a china cabinet. While struggling with the repair, there were times I wished I'd left it on the curb. But staining and seeing the transformation makes the hard part fade into the past. Now when I see it I always think "from swords to plowshares" and wonder if it enjoys holding pottery more than it did weaponry.

I know that every task takes certain skills and strengths, mental and physical, but some are not as hard as you might

My dock is not as easy to move as the modern ones, but to me, it's more beautiful.

think. I just heard a friend raving about how I swam the neighbor's old wooden dock across the lake, in three large sections, when they got a new one. Sure, it took a while, but wood does float, and I love to swim. I felt no stress or danger, since I could have rested any time I wanted, letting the dock support me. But I was too excited to get my "new" dock over to my shore! Years later, when the lake level rose over the dock, I had to move it, waterlogged and with its pilings now attached, about ten feet in toward the shore. After considerable angst and thought, I decided I would try it, a few inches at a time, by holding my breath, standing under the dock, and raising it with my head and

From swords to plowshares, guns to pottery.

hands while I pushed the pilings with my knees. It was a lot harder than floating it across the lake, but it worked. Satisfaction!

I've had to get used to living with "works in progress," since found materials don't always show up on schedule, and new projects often have to wait their turn. My friends are never surprised to see a piece of furniture in my living room awaiting the right stain or upholstery, and they look forward to seeing the dressed-up version—or a replacement. Yes, sometimes I simply change my mind or give up on a project. As I age, I know my ability to do my own fixing and building and maintenance will fade, but also that using those skills will prolong them.

I don't blame anyone for not wanting to do what I do. I share my story to encourage others to try new things even if they seem daunting at first. Or maybe these words will change your perspective the next time one of your modern conveniences breaks down. Instead of the noise of the dishwasher, appreciate the conversation between the table clearer, the washer, and the dryer. Enjoy the whispering swish of an old-fashioned broom more than a squealing electric one, and be grateful for strong arms that are as happy to lift a garage door as push a button. Use a broom or a rake instead of a leaf blower. You'll bring more strength to your body and more quiet to the neighborhood — quiet that may welcome a wild critter or two.

I never had the chance to take shop classes in high school. I began my building projects with no experience and learned everything along the way. How? To my mantra of *"I can think, I can wait, I can fast,"* I added, *"I can read, I can ask, I can do."* Working in libraries taught me that you can learn just about anything if you're willing to read, and that there are several ways to do most projects. So I learned to check a variety of sources and people before deciding on a plan. Then I learned by doing. That's not always easy and it can be frustrating, but in the end it's almost always satisfying. That's when Gershwin's old song comes to mind: "Nice work if you can get it."

Often, a new project is easier because of what I learned on the last project. I don't mean just physical skills, but also patience, perseverance, and problem solving. It's never too late to add those skills to our tool belts. We never know when they might come in handy.

7
Cabins I Have
Known and Loved

When I was a young girl, our family went up to Duluth for a short vacation. The cabin in the woods where we stayed was old, tiny, and rustic, very dark brown and weathered, adorned with vines and serenaded with birdsong. I made a wish to live in one like it when I grew up.

The next cabins that charmed me were at summer camps where I first stayed as a camper, and later as a counselor and lifeguard. Some were log, some just rough-sawn wood, but each came with that special woody cabin smell, the quiet of Northern Minnesota, and the camaraderie of friends. Coming of age there meant independence from home and interdependence with strangers becoming friends. Living with ten girls in a small space meant emphasis on *not* having *things.* All we needed for entertainment during daily quiet time was that big safety pin attaching a length of flat plastic cord to the bunks above our beds. We would fill that time weaving our favorite colors into a lanyard to hold a coveted whistle. We shared responsibilities for housekeeping, cooking, and merrymaking. How could I forget

I built this arbor from dead trees and let the grape vines adorn it. It sets the "up north at the cabin" mood as critters and friends walk through it to the small peninsula that is my home.

those spare and special abodes? They were true to the original purpose of buildings—simply to shelter us for the brief times we could not be out in the real world; exploring, swimming, canoeing, or learning of life (and ghosts!) around a campfire.

My high school sweetheart's family used to take us up to a quaint little boathouse cabin on Gull Lake, near Brainerd, where the loons called and waves lapped at the old stone foundation. I loved waking to the smell of bacon and eggs and filling the days with beach walks and swimming, learning to water ski and play cards. My boyfriend's folks didn't seem to mind packing and hauling meals, laundry, and the boat back and forth in thick traffic every weekend, but it seemed terribly inefficient and expensive to me. That's when I decided the perfect life would be on a lake near the city, even if it wouldn't have quite the magic of living in the wild.

I felt privileged to see true wilderness living when I visited local legend, Billy Needham, in his cabin on a tiny peninsula near Northern Minnesota's glorious Boundary Waters. Both Billy and his home were small, but overflowing with art and stories. Here was a self-sufficient man, living year-round in the wilderness, entertaining himself and his guests as he carved whimsical figures from branches and painted landscapes on the smooth underbellies of shelf fungus. I'd seen hundreds of these on trees but never imagined they would serve as a canvas for a creative soul. I can still hear him call, "Black Duck! Black Duck! Black Duck!" and see his feathered friend glide in for a treat. I was inspired. Even if I couldn't live in the wilderness, I'd want my home to be like Billy's—full of things I had made, and surrounded by nature.

College brought invitations to a friend's cabin, built long ago by people with enough money for two homes and enough sense to build one in the woods. It was large enough to accommodate their extended family—or our rowdy crew of avid smelters.

What is smelting, you ask? For us it was a coming-of-age ritual, and excluded anyone too old, too young, or too sensible to relish the adventure. With only the moon and hissing Coleman lanterns for light and warmth, we set out on the early spring ritual meticulously timed by Mother Nature's drive to reproduce. I stood in the icy stream as it rushed down to Lake Superior, my legs battered by a school of smelt—silvery little fish struggling upstream to spawn. I plunged my bare hand into the dark water and brought up four or five wriggling smelt—much more challenging and fun than scooping them into garbage cans with huge nets. (Some used these then-plentiful smelt as fertilizer. Not us! We ate all we could and froze or pickled the rest.) After an hour or two in the icy stream, we were very glad it was a warm cabin, and not a cold tent, we were returning to.

Well into the next day, I finally woke after our watery midnight safari and began to soak up the ambiance of this extraordinary place. It struck me that these people, who could probably afford any furnishings they wanted, chose the same style that captivated me at that first humble little shack near Duluth. Twig chairs, birchbark lampshades, worn but inviting couches, wood-plank floors softened with old Persian rugs. We chose our crockery from the mix of rugged earthenware bowls, colorful Fiestaware plates, and delicately hand-painted Japanese china. These cast-offs from civilization had become treasures of the cabin, more fitting than any matched sets. The books on the built-in shelves were classics befitting the contemplative nature of the place—Thoreau, Sigurd Olson, Francis Lee

Jaques—or guides to the flora and fauna you might happen upon as you explored the forest and shore. Board games or puzzles replaced the televisions and radios of the city. (Internet? It was not yet a thing!)

The evening campfire, or the fireplace on cold, rainy days, was the heart of the cabin experience. Whether bringing young and old together for stories and songs, or drawing you deeper into your toasty self before snuggling into a cool bed—the gold and blue flames, the primal scent, and the seething red life in the dying coals took you somewhere you needed to go.

The stone fireplace was the soul of the log cabin I rented for most of the seventies. It was an authentic ranger's cabin, taken apart log by log by a woman up north and reassembled (with electricity and plumbing added) in its new home just south of Minneapolis. Suddenly, tiny as it was, it became the preferred location for meetings of all kinds. Men would come to pick me up for a date, walk in the door, pause and ask, "Couldn't we just stay here?" Another movie missed, but I didn't mind. There was a tranquility there that permeated any gathering. Sitting on the shag rug by the fire made short work of getting to know each other, getting through the superficialities, and getting to the core of any conversation.

The first-graders who filled my days with work and wonder were surprised to learn I didn't live at the school. They were even more puzzled when I told them I lived in a log cabin, like Abe Lincoln had. So I invited each class to come for a day. We planned, shopped for, and made our picnic lunch together. We poured plaster into small molds we made in the damp beach

An old, faded snapshot, but wonderful memories of the ranger's cabin I rented for seven years in the seventies. The stone fireplace was the heart of it, but I'm glad it also had a furnace.

My furnishings were perfectly suited to the log cabin, as was my cat, Ashmellow.

sand. I figured I could keep the kids outside most of the day, but they were intrigued by the cabin and explored it thoroughly. (I recently watched a dozen Asian otters chirping and flowing ceaselessly in and out of every corner of their rocky enclosure at the zoo. Make that twenty-four kidlets in a cabin and you get the picture.) One little blond rascal did get stuck between the toilet and vanity, but we managed to extract him without a plumber, and with more laughter than tears. Decades later, the clerk ringing up my groceries, surely in her forties, exclaimed, "Miss Jorgensen! I can still remember when we went to your log cabin!" The memory warmed both her heart and mine.

I spent most of my twenties in that cabin and never tired of seeing how each crafted log fit into the matrix of my home, so when my colleague (and father of one of my students), Roger, invited me to Wisconsin to help them build a cabin from the trees on their family's 200 acres, I jumped at the chance. I managed to strip the bark from only one big log that weekend, yet having Roger call me a "free spirit" and having his father, Stan, admire my strength and enthusiasm for working with my hands left an indelible mark on me. Just working with these industrious people and witnessing their creative skills helped show me who I wanted to be. Years later, they invited me to spend a winter weekend there alone, where I reveled in the finely crafted quilts and exquisitely massive table that Roger's wife, Edie, had made for their hideaway. While there, walking for hours through moonlit snow, I wrote "Turn the World Around," a song about giving kids the experiences and support they need to grow and change the world. I wonder how many kids these days get to sleep in a tent, help build a log cabin, or even discover the strength of their own arms.

The effort it took to peel that single log made me even more awed when I read Laurie Shepherd's book, *A Dreamer's Log Cabin.* This amazing young teacher, writer, and artist built her own log cabin in Northern Minnesota, essentially by hand, eating potatoes and carrots she grew herself. As luck and love would have it, she married Kent, the brother of Julie, who owned "my" log cabin. I relished stories about their pioneering lives. Unlike most people, who think of a cabin as a second home "up at the lake," Laurie and Kent chose to stay there, building on as their family grew to four. When I eventually visited, it had more space and conveniences but had retained the modesty, artistic charm, and practical earthiness of its humble beginning. To my eyes, the dreamer's log cabin was as fascinating and romantic as any castle, but without an ounce of waste or pretense.

When I found and later bought my house here on Sunset Lake, a flood of joyful tears told me I was home, even if it wasn't made of logs. I could finally live in my *own* place at the lake and still be close to family and the richly diverse arts and culture of the Twin Cities. I was glad it had been rebuilt with added insulation and dependable heat, light, and water, but I was intrigued by its childhood as a 1925 country cabin. I decided to honor its simple beginnings by preserving the fieldstone walls and adding as many rustic elements as I could. I stained the cedar siding a deep brown and let grapevines adorn her, reminiscent of that first little shack I was smitten with in Duluth. The intimate conversations of friends and the "sister sessions" I've had here remind me of the secrets shared and glorious laughter at childhood camps. The stone foundation is as lovely and unique as that of the boathouse on Gull Lake. The humble log walls I added, the heat of the wood stove, and every exhilarating plunge into the lake bring me the same joy I felt in my old log cabin.

Of course I know this isn't *everyone's* style. After having me to dinner at his McCastle, a date came here so I could return the favor. He walked into the living room, from where you can see the entire 900 square feet of my house, and asked, "This is it?"

Yes, that *was* it—our second and last date. But he was the exception. And even he was entranced when we canoed at dusk with classical music wafting from my neighbor Rich's beloved piano.

Since Bill and Jane moved in across the lake, they have often shared their exceptional hospitality with me and others by serving delicious dinners in their large, lovely home. Yet when they gave me a tour, they took me up to the third level to show me "the best part of our house—the view of your house." I was

The dark cedar siding and grape vines on my house remind me of the first cabin I stayed in.

flattered and a bit embarrassed, but saw what they meant. Just looking at the simple cottage rising from the naturally flowing land was like a momentary vacation, a step back in time.

How blessed I am to have a home I can enjoy from inside, outside, and across the lake. How wonderful that my friends and I can have very different kinds of homes, while appreciating both. My goal has always been to keep my house as cabiny and my yard as wild as practical, while making both a bit more accessible and beautiful. That means some people wonder why I don't cut down all the grape vines and dead trees, and why I prefer the mixture of clover, plantain, yarrow, daisies, milkweed, and yes, even creeping Charlie in my grass to a monoculture maintained with chemicals. The critters like it, and so do the friends who sigh as they walk under my arbor into Holly's haven to soak up the serenity.

8
From Pigeon Coop to Cozy Cabin

I had fulfilled that wish I made back at the boathouse on Gull Lake—to buy a place that felt like it was up north, but was close to the city—so I figured I could easily forgo vacations. But moving into my dream home added all the responsibilities of property ownership to an already full life. I loved it too much to complain, but I soon found that *living on* the lake was not the same as *going up to* the lake. Instead of hearing just the call of the loons, I heard the call of the house and yard. They had been largely neglected by Bob in his later years and were in serious need of work. LOTS of work. I loved it all, but I felt the need to get away and couldn't afford vacations. I found the answer in my own backyard.

When I bought the house from Bob, he said not to worry about the little old building out back; he'd burn it down before he left. Lowly as it was, I said, "No, let it be." It had started as a single garage. Bob had moved it onto the property and converted it into a pigeon coop and later into a clubhouse for him and his pigeon-racing buddies. With only a few small windows covered in hardware cloth to keep out the raccoons, it was dark and dingy, but it had that woody scent that took me right back

The cozy cabin's cozy kitchen.

This was the garage turned pigeon coop turned clubhouse before I turned it into the cozy cabin.

to my childhood camps. Surely it had another metamorphosis in its future.

Once I'd gotten settled and finished some of the many necessary repairs to the house, I set out to clean up what I had dubbed "the cozy cabin." Scrubbing pigeon poop from the wood floor was a challenge, but that, and pulling the heavy metal screening from the windows, brightened it up a lot. I put a well-worn couch and small table in there, and began to enjoy the quiet and stark simplicity when I needed to "get away."

The real transformation began years later when my neighbor Doug offered me some lovely casement windows salvaged from an old mansion. He seemed to think I could put them in, and I didn't know any better. (This has often been the case in my life.) Being a librarian, I had no excuse not to "look it up." After consulting several books on window framing, asking the clerks at the hardware store, and ruminating, ruminating, ruminating,

I replaced two of the little old windows with the larger, more elegant ones.

Doug stopped by later and complimented me on the fine job. I smiled and thanked him for the windows, the encouragement, and the kudos. Then he added, "Now that you have the flimsy old paneling pulled off that wall, you should really gut it all—insulate and Sheetrock the whole place."

I said no thanks, that was way too much work, and I liked even that old paneling better than drywall. But Doug went on to list the advantages: it would stabilize the old building, make it cooler in the summer and warmer in spring and fall (there was no heat) and make it considerably more fire resistant. "Okay, okay, you're right. But I'm only doing it if I find the insulation and Sheetrock for free, and then I'll need some knotty pine to finish it. I'll have no painted suburban walls in *this* cozy cabin!"

Of course, I soon found plenty of insulation for all four walls and the attic: extra rolls here and there, plus a windfall of pristine pink gold from a house being torn down. The Sheetrock showed up in a dumpster—many perfectly fine sheets, but with two feet cut off the end. Having grown up with a quilting mother, I could certainly deal with that. The plastic vapor barrier, which often escaped from construction sites with the wind, was easy to find.

Thus began a project that snowballed as other things began showing up. When Deb, who had given me the cedar log scraps, offered me a free sliding glass door, I hired Doug to install it in the walkout basement of my house. Then I installed the old one in the cabin, which opened the view of the woods and lake. A huge roll of vinyl wall-covering and rough-sawn cedar planks covered the old ceiling. And yes, the knotty pine I'd insisted on appeared in a huge pile on the curb. Sure, it was cut into four-foot lengths and some were dark and some were light, but Mom was a quilter, remember? The cozy cabin was supposed to be a place to get away, not a never-ending undertaking. But it was serving me well as both.

Though I loved wood floors, the coop's old grooved boards were almost impossible to keep clean, and many scrubbings with bleach failed to revive any beauty they'd once had. The pigeons had really left their mark. So I found some floor paint at the recycling center and hid their secret under emerald green. More recycled paint got mixed into a rustic brown and covered the outside, accented with black to match the house.

After using all the best tongue-and-groove cedar logs for the interior walls of my Up-North Downstairs, I still had quite a pile of scraps left. Clearly there was no choice but to build a six-by-eight-foot "kitchen" onto the cozy cabin. Cement blocks for the foundation, plywood for the floor and roof, and a front door with sidelights all showed up quickly, keeping me busy that summer. A few years later I found a hand-carved door with a leaded glass window on the curb. There was a crack in the etched glass, but I still couldn't resist bringing it home. My book on home repairs said, "There are many projects that are easy. Hanging doors is not one of them." They were right. But it was worth the work. The kitchen's quaintly artistic door and its antique-ish furnishings make it one of my favorite rooms. Like the handcrafted old buildings at historical sites, it makes me feel at home.

I added two more of my old cabin windows to the main room and wondered what the rangers saw through them perhaps a

Would the homing pigeons who lived here recognize their old coop now?

century earlier. Adding a big window in the west wall gave me a view of the sunset through the trees.

Free furniture started showing up, and it's been a challenge not to let it crowd the cabin and ruin its simplicity. When a simple wooden futon frame seemed more fitting than the white hide-a-bed I'd been using, I "altered" my mattress to fit it and disassembled the hide-a-bed for recycling. Rainbows of antique trade blankets and quilts made their way from Indian, Mexican, and Scandinavian hands by way of the trash to my little cabin. They add a special warmth to chilly nights.

As my little hermitage took shape and I began spending nights in the cabin, I loved listening to the hooting of owls, the howling of coyotes, and the rain on the tin roof. With all those added windows and doors, I felt like I was sleeping outside, cooled by the mist on the wind and sweetened by the intoxicating fragrance of plum blossoms.

The occasional midnight walks up to the "big" house to use the bathroom weren't really bad—only seventy-five steps—and were often rewarded by a glimpse of a deer snacking at the salad bar I thought was my garden or a 'possum checking out the veggie scraps in my compost pile. But there was still that small stack of cedar logs, leftovers from the basement walls and the cabin kitchen. So I had to build an outhouse, just for fun. Mom joined in, adding a coat of green paint to the two little found windows that fit just right and provided light and breeze, even in this thirty-by-thirty-inch one-holer.

When neighbor Donna offered me her old dock, I knew it would make the perfect cabin porch. I found some old cement footings and spent an afternoon getting it level and secure. A roof extension has been in the plans for a while, but I'm hesitant to block out the part of the sky that speaks to me as I sit in the rocker outside my cozy cabin, reflecting and writing. I'd hate to miss an eagle!

As I spent more time on that porch, I found myself wishing it were just two feet wider than the four-foot dock. The next

I love writing in the quiet of this deck made of docks. I rarely use the outhouse, but it has come in handy, especially if I'm sleeping out there in a rainstorm and nature calls along with the owls and coyotes.

week, there it was, a two-by-fifteen-foot, well-made dock with a "free" sign. Neighbors helped me put it on the roof of my car. Once I got it home, it took only a few hours to level the land, find the right stones or logs for support, and muscle the dock into place. *Voila!* I had my new, expanded porch.

I should admit, in the interest of full disclosure, that renovating the cabin was a bit like having a baby (from what I've heard). There was pain, and swearing, and times when I thought *This is impossible!* and wondered how I ever got myself into this ridiculous predicament. So when I give my talks about how

Nearly everything I needed to renovate the cabin was rescued from the trash. Not all of the tasks were fun, but the result was worth the work.

The cozy cabin will always be a work in progress, but its salvaged furnishings make it a comfortable and special retreat.

much I loved the project, I include the picture Mom took of me on a ladder, dripping with sweat, bandanna and goggles and gas mask to protect me from the obnoxious fiberglass insulation (did I really call it "pink gold"???!) as I crawled into the 90 degree, two-foot-high attic. Thank goodness for the amnesia that ripens with the fruit of our labors—be it bouncing baby or cozy cabin!

I'm glad to have a radio and CD player in the cabin, for the music and stories were an integral part of the building process. The friendly sounds helped me carry the heavy loads, the rhythm of drums guided my hands as I scrubbed, painted, nailed, and sawed. I've been offered TVs and know I could watch movies there on my computer, but I refuse these distractions as I refuse to let this sacred space become cluttered. Dusty, yes; cluttered, no.

I do sometimes bring my laptop out to the cabin to write, though writing in my journal by the kerosene lamp feels much more fitting to the space. I may go there when I'm sad to figure things out or ask for guidance from the wise woods. I always smile and say hello as I enter—because my cozy cabin makes me happy. There is a special peace there, perhaps because of all the life around it, perhaps from all the hard work I put into it. Or perhaps the cozy cabin's many comfortable imperfections help me to be comfortable with my own. That's a quality that has value, even if you're not lucky enough to have a cabin, and even if you prefer city life.

Have you noticed the trend of lighting up the outside walls of very large houses, making them look even bigger, sometimes

The glow from within my house is doubly enchanting when reflected in the lake.

Parthenon-like, at night? There's the antithesis of a cabin. I heard someone say, while fishing at dusk and being irritated by such an ostentatious specter, some simple but profound words:

"The glow is supposed to come from within."

9
Oh, the Things You'll Find at the Curbside Boutique

I've told you a lot about the riches I've found on the curb and in dumpsters, and I'm certainly grateful for what I've been able to do with the castoffs of other people. But there's a dark side to this story.

On May Day, 2008, I found a new American flag, still folded in its box, in a pile of trash on the curb. The enclosed instructions for flag etiquette said, "The flag should never touch anything beneath it, such as the ground, the floor, or water." Does that include trash?

I rescued it, of course. We've heard debates for years about whether desecrating the flag should be a crime or is protected by the constitution as free speech, but tossing one on a trash pile seems to be an act of negligence, if not actual disrespect.

And what about the brand-new clothes, cookware, books, and other articles that people casually dispose of? I'll bet they'd be appreciated by families struggling to make ends meet. What about the quality coats I've found on the curbside that could be keeping people warm, but are bound instead for the burgeoning

None of this furniture was good enough to donate to Bridging or Goodwill, but it was perfect to create this outdoor room overlooking my lake.

During curbside cleanup days, this scene is repeated, house after house, block after block, mile after mile, week after week. But it also illustrates what gets thrown out in neighborhoods that don't sponsor the cleanups.

landfills? I am amazed to see the many gifts, given in love, hope, pride, or obligation, that end up hidden in black plastic bags on the curb. Perhaps they weren't exactly right, or the recipient already had three of them. But why aren't they being donated to the church rummage sale, the Salvation Army, or the dozens of other thrift stores and charities?

The good news is that I'm not the only one shopping—and rescuing—at the Curbside Boutique. The annual pickup days in many communities attract more and more "junkers" from all walks of life. When I found a group of women rescuing goods from a mountain of trash and asked if I could take their picture to use in my talks, they smiled and posed happily. We all agreed that if there was any embarrassment due, it should belong to those who threw out perfectly good items instead of donating them to those in need.

No one was embarrassed to be rescuers. We agreed only those throwing out usable things should be embarrassed. (By the way, I'm still using that gray vacuum cleaner.)

In the library where I worked, I saw people from around the world emailing home every day. I wondered if any reported seeing their neighbors carelessly tossing out a colorful blanket from South America, a TV from Japan, an exquisite brass vase from India, or a hand-knitted Norwegian sweater. The thought of it embarrassed me.

I am happy when I find something I need or something unique or antique. But more often I am sad to find furniture and clothing that was perfectly usable—until soaked with rain or deliberately smashed. I am torn when I find things that are

Right in the community where this furniture is headed for the landfill, there is a wonderful non-profit called Bridging. It provides donated furniture and household goods (and hope!) to families and individuals transitioning out of homelessness and poverty.

useful and beautiful, because I can't rescue and find homes for everything. And I'm frustrated when I come upon the plethora of plastic objects, large and small, with so little true beauty or integrity or usefulness that I wonder why they were produced in the first place. Soon they'll be headed to the landfills, where they'll lie for decades, if not centuries, without even the humble hope of decomposing into life-giving compost.

I can't enjoy scavenging without acknowledging that there is something terribly wrong here. While significant parts of the planet are struggling to meet their basic needs — food, water, shelter, clothing, education — the biggest concern of many Americans is what to do with all their stuff. When their desperate attempts to organize it fail, they move on to plan B: "Just get it out of here!" with little thought given to where it came from, where it's going, or why they bought it in the first place. I must admit I have more understanding of that feeling since dealing

I often find warm, quality clothing in the trash.

with emptying my parents' house. It's a huge task, and one that overwhelms me and many of my fellow baby boomers. But I don't believe the trash is the answer.

Certainly redistribution of goods could solve problems on both sides of the scale. I once found an official Los Angeles Dodgers jacket, wool and leather still in good shape, in a curbside pile. *Someone must want this,* I thought. I gave it to my neighbor to see if she could sell it on eBay. It didn't bring in a lot of money, but it went to Russia! What a thrill it was to know the jacket I'd rescued from the dump was being loved by someone on the other side of the planet.

An old friend once said to me, "If everyone lived like you do, our economy would collapse." It's a common argument, but I don't buy it. The reverse is more likely to be true. Consider this: If everyone lives to shop, and suppliers of goods are concerned only with profits, converting precious natural resources into disposable products, our *ecology* will collapse. Then surely, so shall the economy. Yet as local and global ecosystems and

I suspect these Beanie Babies were bought with the belief that their value as collectibles would skyrocket, yet they ended up on the curb, still in pristine shape with the tags on. I gave them to a friend who gave them to a friend who took them to Africa for kids who may never have had a toy.

economies deteriorate, many still see their only hope in "consumer demand"—which is usually stimulated by throwing away the old stuff to make way for the *new* stuff. We might do better with an economy based on fewer but better and more durable products. Such an approach would free us from the romance of the "next new thing" and the need to work overtime to scrape together the funds to buy it.

Don't get me wrong. I'm all in favor of technological innovation. Three cheers to the entrepreneurs who are designing tomorrow's windmills, solar panels, and hybrid cars. But there are countless other opportunities to change the world while making money. One lifesaving example is a simple straw that filters and purifies water, allowing people in underdeveloped countries to drink from unclean sources. Solar technology is now being incorporated into roof shingles, and even paint, making the sun's power more affordable and accessible. High-density hydroponic farming holds a water-saving, pesticide-free promise. If these examples sound boring to you, check out Harvard's yearly Ig Nobel Prize, a competition for achievements that first make people laugh — and then make them think.

Scientist Elena Bodnar, after participating in the evacuation of children from the deadly gasses at the Chernobyl nuclear catastrophe, won an Ig Noble prize in public health for developing the Emergency Bra. Seriously. A woman wearing one can remove it without otherwise disrobing and convert it quickly into two face masks that can save lives. It even comes in black, white, and red! (What if every woman in Syria wore one?) Surely this kind of creative commodity can propel economies more sustainably than the use-it-and-throw-it fads flowing in and out of stores month after month.

I have great faith in the power of technological innovation. After all, it is a gift of the gods! Prometheus stole fire from the heavens and gave technology to humanity. But let's not forget that Zeus understood the potentially devastating powers of that gift. He saw the chaos that ensued when community was disrupted, and he bestowed upon us two remedies: justice and reverence. Zeus knew that without these, technology would fail. There's a reason this Greek myth has lasted for so many centuries. As both constructive and destructive technological powers mushroom, we need, more than ever, the scales of justice and the balm of reverence.

And how about a little more old-fashioned honesty? Recently I came home with a bag of cosmetics, cleaners, medicines, printer ink, spices, and dried fruit. (Yes, there are a few things I don't make or buy used.) As I opened my purchases, I found almost every box was about twice the size of the product inside. Besides making me feel duped, it made me sad to think of the resources wasted in producing, transporting, and displaying all of this oversized packaging. (The EPA says that *one-third* of consumer trash sent to landfills is packaging.) It also makes fresh produce and non-processed, minimally packaged food — where what you see is what you get — more appealing. Besides the peace of mind this visibility provides, these are often the more healthful, economic, and earth-friendly choices.)

Rummage sales have the same advantage. The deceptive packaging is long gone, and someone else has paid for its disposal. This is part of the reason (along with recycling, donating, and composting) that I get by with on-call garbage collection. I average only two or three pickups a year. Do I have a trash compactor? Well, sort of. I pack what little trash I have into my empty cartons, reducing the size, the smell, and the chance that anything will escape on the wind. I guess I pick up more "trash" from the curb than I have picked up from my house!

Are we being coddled into losing our ability to fix things? One of my rare but thoroughly worthwhile new purchases was a good snow shovel with a bent handle that minimizes back strain. Now *there's* an innovation worth buying, especially if you have 100 yards of driveway and live in the Snow Belt, as I do. But after years of use, the plastic top of the handle split and came off the metal tube. Bummer. I *had* to have a shovel—*now*. So I had to go buy a new one, right? Gluing plastic to metal and

Fix-it Clinics—a very bright idea! That's my old lamp. Everyone I met there was as helpful and friendly as this guy, who fixed it with the tools, parts, and expertise needed.

expecting it to hold up to many pounds of pressure in subzero temperatures would surely be a waste of time and effort. Right?

But I *never* rush out to buy anything. I always take a moment to *think*. I knew I must have a clamp somewhere in my collection of "save it just in case you need it" stuff. Sure enough, I did, right in the box labeled "clamps." It was worth a try. I brought the shovel in, glued it, and clamped it. The next day's snowfall provided the test, and the little old clamp passed. I got many more years of use out of that shovel before that plastic handle crumbled under the clamp. Oh, dear. I went to buy a new shovel, but they were *all plastic*. How could that be an improvement? I'd seen too many broken ones to believe those scoops were made for Minnesota winters. In desperation, I brought my shovel to the local hardware store. The replacement "D handles" on the shelf didn't fit. Seeing my disappointment, the clerk went in the back room and found a perfectly good D handle he'd salvaged from an older shovel. It fit! I was thrilled. He made a few bucks, and two things stayed out of the landfill. That was years ago. I'm still using that shovel, and I smile every time I do.

I understand that not everyone wants to or can repair things, or is willing to keep a supply of great little fixer thingies on hand. I also understand that many products these days lack the simplicity to make them fixable by anyone but a highly trained professional. And I appreciate that these skilled people should be appropriately paid for their labor and expertise. The dilemma arises when the cost of a new whatever is less than the cost to fix the old one—if you consider only the cost to the consumer, and not to the planet! Whether planned or not, obsolescence is the norm. But I believe there is a beautiful equation, some golden ratio just around the corner that will provide us with useful goods that are efficient, durable, and repairable; will encourage old-fashioned problem-solving skills at home, and will put more people to work repairing and refurbishing. Then fewer things will be hauled to landfills. I am greatly encouraged by the communities now holding fix-it clinics. People bring items needing repair to a center where volunteers show them how to fix them!

I grew up watching *Superman* on TV. Were we naïve to think our superhero could save us using "Truth, Justice, and the American Way"? If we really demanded truth in advertising, wouldn't most ads begin with "You don't really need this, but . . ."? If we really believed in justice, would we keep buying and buying brand names so the CEOs of large corporations can be rewarded with four or five *hundred* times as much in salaries as the people do who actually produce the goods? Is it time to recapture our founding values and redefine "The American Way"?

I doubt very much that the person who put that flag on the trash pile was intending to make a political statement. But I heard one, loud and clear. Daily, I hear people thank our military men and women for sacrificing so that we can live the way we do. Is this lifestyle worth their sacrifice?

While we demand respect for our beloved flag, let us not forget to respect the earth and all its inhabitants. The laws of nature strive for equilibrium. An out-of-balance world is a dangerous place.

10

A Unicorn of my Own

In 2005, our president was talking about America becoming an "ownership society." But that wasn't why I was about to pay off the mortgage on my house. I didn't like paying interest, so my plan had always been to pay it off as soon as I could. I had never spent much on vacations, restaurants, or other luxuries, but I would forgo even more until my house was my own. I knew people who cared not a wink about owning a house, much less paying it off. They relished the freedom of renting, of traveling, even living in a truck. I knew a woman who lived in a tiny hut hidden in a park preserve, dug into the ground and covered with old tarps and a torn wading pool. She seemed to find as much joy in the images of frolicking blue dolphins surrounding the clear plastic window as some of my other friends might find in expensive new draperies. I understood the choices of each, but none of these were for me. I wanted the freedom of being grounded. I hadn't calculated the tens of thousands of dollars in interest I saved by paying the loan off early, but the emotional security I felt was immeasurable.

I'll never forget walking into the credit union to make my last payment. It felt surreal that everyone else looked so normal, so casual, when this great event was about to take place! I walked up to the window, asked for the final amount, and wrote out the check. I raised my arms in the air and said, quietly but emphatically, "I own my house!"

I felt a little silly, thinking the pretty young woman at the window saw this every day, but the look on her face told me otherwise. I was holding back tears, and I think she felt the same. She looked into my eyes and said, "I want to do that!"

I said, "Do it. If I did, you can. Make the sacrifices. It's worth it."

I stepped out the door as the tears came, pure joy taking my breath away. When I could see clearly enough to drive, I went home — to *my* home. I touched *my* earth. I looked at each rock, each tree, with new eyes and new responsibility. These were *my* rocks and *my* trees. The shoreline I'd worked to keep natural was mine. And yes, the dreaded buckthorn, poison ivy, and reed canary grass were mine too, but I loved them all. I knew that all these treasures, and especially my house, would, like children, demand my care and attention for decades to come. But they would also be my refuge, my shelter, the acre of earth that would keep me grounded and safe. No one could take that away from me.

So who was I to question the wisdom of the "ownership society?" And I didn't until it became clear to me (and many others) that millions of people who thought they owned their homes really didn't. The only thing they owned was their debt. Some had been the victims of predatory lending. Others had simply bought the "common wisdom" that house values would continue to rise forever. The easy availability of home equity loans tempted them to buy flashy boats, add on three-season porches, or splurge on romantic cruises. Why not?

Then the housing market crashed and the foreclosure notices went up. I was afraid for friends who feared losing their homes, and sad for those who did. But I didn't know what to say when they asked, "How did you know you should pay off your house?"

I am relatively naive when it comes to high finance, but I knew there was a big difference between *owning* a house and *owing on* a house. Sometimes it works to follow your gut — and your heart.

Yet it's so easy to confuse love and ownership. Do you just *love* this? Just *love* that? So you just *gotta have* it? That's what the media will tell you.

When I got my first full-time teaching job and was looking for a place to rent, a woman named Julie called me to come and see the log cabin that was connected to their house by a hallway. When she opened the door, I told her I didn't want to look at it. I could tell immediately that I would love it. I was also sure it would be too expensive, especially since it was on a lake. "Oh," she replied, "is $100 a month too much?"

Okay, so that *was* in 1974, and it *was* just a tiny old ranger's cabin, but that modest rent still felt like a gift. I loved that cabin, and grew to love the family at the other end of the hall. We shared the yard, the beach, and our lives. Little Laura put me on her kindergarten family tree and cried when Julie told her I wasn't really her big sister. Seven years later, when they needed the space and I had to move on, I understood—but I cried, too.

My heart was broken again thirty years later, when I heard the property had been sold and the cabin would be disassembled and put in a wood chipper. It seemed an irreverent end to this noble bit of history we had shared. I tried for weeks to find someone to move it elsewhere, just to preserve it, but to no avail. I salvaged what I could from both the cabin and connected house, but couldn't bear to be there for the end.

I felt a little sad when I ran across a picture of four-year-old Laura with Mom, me, and my cat Ashmellow sitting in the log cabin. But there was another, of grown-up Laura with Mom, me, and my cat Spike sitting by the log wall in my current house. That was when I realized that I still had what was important about the cabin. Yes, I loved its massive logs and stone fireplace, but the relationships I formed there were also precious. Sharing playful swims, fireside chats, gardening, and responsibilities with my landlords had made the cabin special.

Julie and her husband Curt visited me a few years ago and were tickled to see remnants of their house and cabin here: the iron railing Curt had made by hand, the pine boards on my ceiling ("I made many trips to the lumber store to pick out the best ones!" he recalled), three sturdy shelves that keep my basement organized, the window shutters that became a gate to keep old dogs and young kids from falling down my intriguing spiral staircase. The old windows with heavy iron hinges held memories of the cabin for all of us. Beyond saving me money and sparing the materials from the bulldozer, salvaging these bits of our shared past strengthened the bond between us. A bond of memories, but also of values: respect for honest work and simple, handsome, useful things. A bond we might have missed if I had owned that cabin instead of renting it from them for seven special years.

That old log cabin was very small. Looking back, it was just small enough not to rob me of too much precious time. I'm grateful to have more room now, since my life has grown and I need space to accommodate more projects and friends. But

I'm very aware that the responsibility of caretaking grows in proportion to what you own. Cleaning, maintaining, storing, and finding! There's a delicate balance required to keep things from owning *you*. Often the thing that is rented or shared is not quite as heavy as that which is owned and it rarely takes up as much space in your home, garage, head, or heart.

You've probably heard the one about George, the ever-borrowing neighbor who asks Henry if he'll be using his shovel that day. "Sorry, George, but I'll be using it all day," replies Henry, hoping to deter George. "Oh, then you won't be using your fishing pole. Mind if I borrow it?" Sometimes good fences do make good neighbors, but I suspect sharing has made more friends than enemies. I can't imagine how I'd have built all that I have around here without borrowing my generous neighbors' tools. There are so many things that we use only on occasion. Do we each really need to own them? True, we are addicted to convenience, but with just a little *thinking, waiting, and fasting,* shared goods can save a lot of money and resources, while helping people form new connections with each other.

A case in point: at a class on buckthorn control, I was introduced to the Weed Wrench, a fabulous tool for pulling out the invasive trees. A nearby community had even started lending out the tool. Soon afterward I announced at a neighborhood picnic that I planned to buy one, and asked if anyone wanted to go in on it. Several of my neighbors did. We split the $180 cost and have shared this sturdy tool and our buckthorn battles ever since.

I'm happy to see the growing interest in community gardening. So many who don't have the space to garden still recognize the value of homegrown organic produce, not to mention the

My buckthorn battles would be hopeless without the borrowed tools and crews of smiling young people from the University YMCA.

great exercise provided by dealing with dirt. I'd love to see as many friendships budding over shared beets and corn as there are at expensive coffee shops.

Sometimes we end up sharing things we wouldn't expect to.

I got to know the lake I live on now by house-sitting for Rich, who had lived on its shore for decades. I was happy to watch his house in the woods with his yellow Lab, Teddy, and his orange tabby cat, Peaches. Teddy and I quickly fell in love, and I looked forward to walking him as much as spending time at beautiful Sunset Lake. Years later, when I bought my house, it took only a week for Teddy to discover his way around the lake to my door. I swear he did doggy cartwheels on my deck when he saw me in the window. I was just as happy. Mom had said I should get a dog when I moved out there, but we both realized my schedule wasn't really conducive to that level of responsibility. So Teddy stepped up to the plate. Though he dearly loved Rich, he loved me too, and began alternating nights there and here. Rich, though he missed Teddy on my nights, generously allowed us our love affair, often introducing me as "Ted's girlfriend."

When a carpet-cleaning truck backed over Teddy as he approached to greet the visitor, it was the start of a trying, but bonding chapter in our lives. Teddy was fourteen — very old for a Lab — and now

Rich and Teddy working together in the garden.

his hip was broken. We'd all known older people for whom that was a death sentence. But even the vets at the university said there was something special about him, and their hopeful prognosis proved true. Teddy's surgery went well, and I slept on Rich's basement floor for the first few nights, there to help Teddy outside for his frequent pees. We cheered when he was finally able to lift his leg and "pee like a man" again. His recovery was long, but complete, and his joy at running through the garden again assured us it had all been worthwhile. In his fifteenth year, he had the happiest birthday party I've ever seen, attended by twenty-four people and three dogs. Even Gentle Doctor Jenny, his vet since he was a pup, came to celebrate. Ted was a gracious host and greeted everyone with his well-known smile. I'm sure his wagging tail was tired by the end of the day.

I was there for Teddy when he needed me, and he returned the favor. That fall, Rich was torn from his marvelous garden by a stroke. When the nurses heard that Teddy was not himself, they let us sneak him into the hospital. There at Rich's bedside, he licked his hand and said goodbye. Knowing how strong our bond was, Rich's wife said, "He's yours now."

Ted came home with me that night and never went back. With my "ownership" of Ted came the added responsibility and cost, but it didn't change our relationship. We had both lost a precious friend and depended on the love between us to hold us up. Teddy lived to seventeen and a half before joining his beloved Rich. He had never been confined by chain or fence, but was free to go where he wished and love whom he loved. Clearly, he never confused ownership and love, and he taught me the same.

Dad always said that a cat's independence made its love more special. When a cat bonds with you, it's not just because you're part of the pack. He knows you don't really own him, but he just might let you into his world if he respects you. I "owned" a handsome green parakeet as a child, and I loved him. There's a different kind of thrill when a vulnerable wild bird wraps its delicate toes trustingly around my finger. As a rule, I don't believe in interfering with nature. More often than not, injured critters either recover on their own, or make a good meal for a hungry predator. But when a naturalist friend taught me how to help a bird breathe after an unfortunate encounter with a window, I had to try it. I gently cupped the bird in my hands, tilting its breast upward in a natural position. Sure enough, it seemed to help open the airway. The birds I've rescued since then have all stood freely on my finger for a while after catching their breath. A black-and-white warbler rose from this strange perch to hover and chirp a sentence to my face before landing back on my finger. A robin even flew away, then came back and rested on my shoulder. (Honest!) That took *my* breath away. To me, these close encounters speak, more than any statistics, of the sacred and irreplaceable nature of wildlife.

Those few ounces of wild songbird bring the same quiet thrill to my heart that I felt years ago in a delightful friendship with a thousand-pound critter—an untrained young thoroughbred

This cedar waxwing and olive-sided flycatcher somehow hit the window together, but recovered and stayed awhile before flying off.

horse, appropriately named Imp. She wasn't mine, but she would run across the pasture to meet me—except for the time she stood at the far end, head down, not moving. I worried that she was ill, until I came close enough to see that she was staring at her lost halter there on the ground. I guess she was tired of her less-observant human friend walking around the field looking for the thing, so she decided not to move until I found it and picked it up. Then there was the time my godson Matt and I found the gate left open. It must have been open all morning, but Imp had no reason to leave the paddock until we were there to chase her back in—what a fun game! There is something in

My friendship with Mary grew each time we shared our love of the outdoors on her wonderful horses.

the personalities of untrained horses, like those of wild birds, that is warm and funny and exhilarating, if unpredictable.

But had it not been for my friend Mary sharing her horses with me, I wouldn't know the exhilaration of riding Bo—a horse that *is* trained, and one, as Mary says, with whom I have mutual respect. Cantering over grassy hills together makes Mary and me feel like the teenagers we were when we first met. I occasionally help her with chores and throw some money her way for hay and gas, but I can never repay her for the hours of friendship, joy, and even free counseling I've received from this wise and always uplifting psychologist. Owning my own horse would have robbed me of all that.

Bo lives an hour away, and I no longer live near Imp, so I was happy that my neighbor Pat had horses I might be able to visit. Just seeing these beautiful creatures in a pasture enriches my day. I had divided my hostas to share with Pat, but thought I'd better ask about the new horses before walking through her pasture with the plant. "Oh, they'll just run away," she said. "They're wild today and didn't even come when I brought their hay."

She was right; they ran as I approached from the woods. So I used the body language I'd learned from reading about various "horse whisperers." I always took that stance when around deer, elk, or horses, just to reassure them. After leaving the hosta at the house, I came back through the pasture, again angling my shoulders, dipping my chin, and licking my lips: horse language for "I'm not a predator, I just want to eat grass, like you do."

As I crossed the field, Sunny surprised me by walking up behind me. I wasn't usually nervous around horses, but I was cautious, especially knowing he was an untrained mustang, born of a wild-caught mother and adopted on Pat's trip out West. When the beautiful white horse placed his head on my shoulder and walked across the field with me, I thought — *Oh, I guess we're friends!*

That became an understatement. I loved walking through the park to the pasture to visit and scratch Sunny behind the ears. But that fall Sunny and his friends needed more than petting. The field was besieged by burdock, turning tails and manes into tangles of stubborn burrs. Burdock may get credit for being the inspiration for Velcro, and its root is a nutritious staple in Japan; but in a horse pasture, it's a terrible pestilence. I pulled as many burrs as I could, and the three horses began to compete for my attention. I started bringing Teddy's undercoat rake, which worked as well on the burrs as it had on his shedding fur.

One day as I approached Sunny, I swore he had become a unicorn. His forelock (the mane which should have hung gracefully over his forehead) was plastered by burrs into a perfect, if torturous horn. I laughed, but then imagined how awful it must have felt as the burrs worked their way into tighter and tighter knots. I was determined to rescue him, but even trained horses are often very sensitive about that area, and he was especially so. I patiently pulled a few burrs, scratching and softly reassuring him. "Trust me, Sunny. You'll feel so much better if you let me get those nasty things out." But he kept backing away.

After several minutes I wondered if this was futile, but then he got it. He suddenly understood and lowered his head to me. He posed there motionless as I separated the hair and combed out the burrs. When his mane was finally freed, soft and white, and my unicorn was once again a horse, he raised his head and gazed at me with unmistakable love in his eyes. I returned the same. We had bonded.

Later I scolded him for nibbling at my shoes, because no one likes a mouthy horse. But when I realized he was pulling burrs from my shoelaces, I remembered that horses bond by grooming, so I couldn't complain when he returned my favor.

When Pat's life took some unexpected turns, she sadly told me she had to move and find new homes for the horses. I understood but was devastated. I tried to think of people in the area who might want them, so I could still see Sunny. Friends said there must be some way for me to keep him. After all, I loved him. But that's the thing about love. Real love means wanting and doing what's best for the one you love. I believed that Sunny loved me and I was good for him. But he needed a trainer. A *good* trainer. Horses are herd animals and are not happy when kept in isolation. If I boarded him elsewhere, I knew I'd be frustrated and torn between him and my many other obligations. I didn't have the skill, pasture, income, nor the time he needed for a good life—the life he deserved.

So I had to be happy when Pat said she found someone to take him—to Florida.

It was winter, and I worried about him going south in his winter coat. He was trailer-shy, and I worried about how he would endure those fifteen hundred miles. I told myself that most horsemen knew that "gentling" a horse was much more effective than "breaking" him. But I worried most of all that Sunny's new owner, unknown to me, might be some macho man who had something to prove by breaking a "wild" mustang.

I never did run into the guy as he worked with Sunny,

preparing him for the trip, but Pat assured me he was a kind and effective trainer. I continued to visit when I could, even if only late at night. We weren't sure when they were leaving, so each time I came through the woods I held my breath as I reached the pasture, and was overjoyed when Sunny appeared in the moonlight. Even without his horn, he was as handsome and magical as any unicorn could be.

On one of these visits, as I stood facing Sunny and stroking his neck, he reached his massive head over my shoulder, as he often did. But this time, he lowered his head along my back and pulled me into his breast, so strongly that it frightened me for a moment and I pulled away. But seeing nothing but gentleness in his eye, I thought in amazement, *I think he just hugged me!*

I came back the next day, stroked him again, and softly asked, "Can I have a *gentle* hug?"

He gave me one—deliberate and firm, but just a little gentler than before. Three more days he hugged me, each a precious memory. But he also sometimes walked away, seemingly telling me it was time to separate, that he had a new person in his life and he would be just fine.

Then one night I came and he was gone. I wept.

It's tempting to believe that owning follows love, and is the bastion against loss. But that is as mythical as a unicorn. Ownership will not ensure love, any more than true love requires ownership.

I loved a horse and my heart broke. But had I owned him, my heart still would have broken, as his owner Pat's surely did. Parting with a beloved or being together until death, love inevitably leads to loss. But if we dare to love and are lucky, our hearts heal, and become stronger, bigger, and more grateful. I was

blessed by and will always be thankful for the time I had with Sunny, even if the thought of him in the moonlight still moistens my eyes.

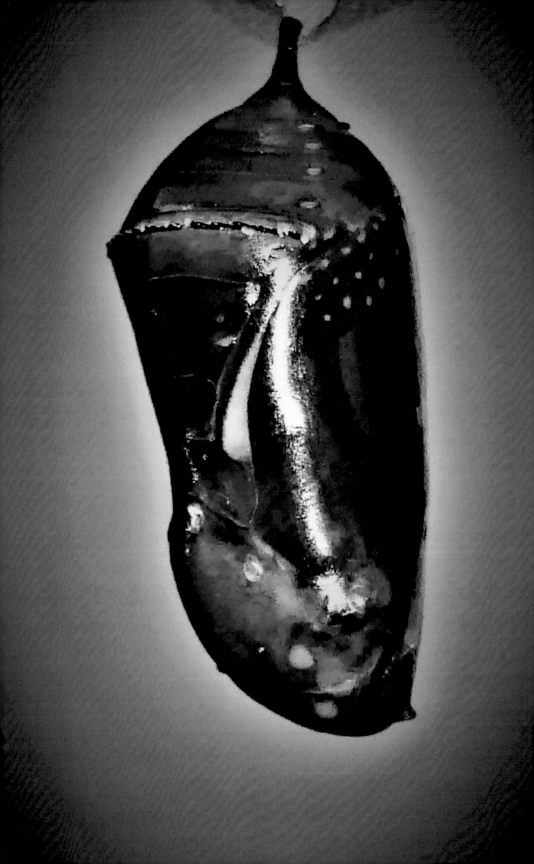

11

The Real Dirt on Dirt

Some might roll their eyes at the thought that Teddy really smiled, or that Sunny really hugged me, or that a robin really came back and perched on my shoulder. But not those who have lived with dogs. Not those, like the Persian poet Rumi, who know that "The wind of heaven is that which blows between a horse's ears." Nor those, like B.B. King, whose solitary childhood days taught them that stillness draws in gentle friends in fur and feathers. King was not a bit surprised that the black-and-white warbler I rescued hovered and "spoke" to me. "Of course," B.B. said. "He was thanking you."

My sixth-grade teacher asked us to write an essay on how language separates humans from all other animals. I struggled and finally told her I couldn't do that, because we didn't really know if other animals had languages. Perhaps we just hadn't learned theirs. She said, "Fine — write on that." I did and got an A+. But I never stopped studying the question of what makes us human — language, tools, self-awareness, art, compassion, imagination, altruism? One by one, these theories have been debunked by both simple and scientific observation.

Since Jane Goodall's discovery of chimps using sticks to gather food, primates have been observed using tools in twenty-two different ways. Alex the African grey parrot understood arithmetic. A border collie named Chaser learned 1,022 words. Even if that doesn't qualify as language, I'm impressed. Experts no longer doubt what animal lovers have always known — animals love us back and feel many other emotions.

I'm not sure I'd call it love, but two sunfish in my lake are definitely my friends. I know it sounds ridiculous, but hear me out. I wondered at it myself two summers ago when a green sunfish made a nest by my dock. That's not unusual. The males are notorious for guarding their nests, but there was something about the way he looked at me. Soon he was letting me pet him. When he showed up last year and acted the same, I offered him the Japanese beetles I pulled off my flowers. He was so excited his orange highlights almost glowed. That seemed to cement the friendship. I named him Greenie so I'd remember his species, since I never knew much about fish. When he showed up the third year, there was a smaller fish with him who was just as friendly. I noticed he used only his left pectoral fin. Eventually the right one healed and has a scar now. That makes positive identification easy, but it's usually behavior that helps me tell one animal from another.

The advantages of a wild pet are obvious: no walking, litter box, or vet bills. But be warned. It hurts your heart when your friend shows up with a torn lip. That's happened twice with Greenie. The second time, he stared at me a long time before he dared come close. It took a beetle treat to regain his trust. I don't blame him. Letting me pet him and rubbing against my leg is one thing. Being held while a hook is twisted from your mouth is another. I still eat fish, but it's different now. I always hope the wild-caught salmon in my freezer were caught

Greenie often rubs against my leg and lets me pet him. When Greenie gets excited over Japanese beetles his pelvic fins get a little more orange.

Spot likes oatmeal better than beetles. When the light hits Spot's right pectoral fin his scars show up — positive identification.

Thanks to Roger for capturing this shot of Greenie and Spot coming to me. My friend Carol thinks the fish are comfortable with me because I swim in their world every day.

humanely and the farmed fish had good lives. Then I wonder if someone is missing a friend or relative. Greenie comes and goes now, but Spot (named for the spot on his dorsal fin) has oatmeal with me just about every morning.

I understand why people might be skeptical about "my" fish. I remember hearing, as a child, that fish couldn't feel pain, much less anything else. Even I wondered if I was just the "human at the dock" and this was their territory. That changed the day I took my daily swim and decided to sit on a log at the other end of the lake and watch the sunset. It was lovely. Then I looked down and saw someone looking up at me. Spot? Really? I put my hand in and he came and nuzzled it, and I saw the white scar that proved it was him. Oh, my goodness. If you are still rolling your eyes, check out the study at Oxford and Queensland Universities that showed fish can recognize a face among forty-four others and remember it for at least six months!

Of course we differ from our nonhuman friends, and excel in many areas they don't. But the reverse is also true. To keep insisting on our superiority seems silly and egocentric to me.

Meanwhile, careful study of other species (before they disappear!) often yields unforeseen rewards for our own health and technology. On PBS's *Nova — Making Stuff Smarter*, I saw a robot capable of climbing a wall thanks to the study of the gecko's feet, and a surface that doesn't let bacteria grow that was modeled after the skin of sharks. The technology that makes cars stop on their own to avoid collisions was inspired by the eyes and neurons of a locust. Think of the implications of really understanding how the Alaskan wood frog survives through the winter by freezing solid. Even the humble woolly-bear caterpillar can freeze and live through up to fourteen arctic winters

Many of us grew up playing with woolley bear caterpillars, but who knew they could freeze solid and later morph into an Isabella tiger moth?

before morphing into the Isabella tiger moth. Even more shocking to me was learning that monarch butterflies remember things they were taught when they were caterpillars, even though they appear to be just "soup" when in the chrysalis! Surely there are lifesaving discoveries waiting to be made from all these unique powers.

On the other hand, I finally heard of one "ability" that truly seems unique to man: only *we* create true waste. Other beings consume resources, use them and leave by-products that other organisms can use in a marvelously efficient circle of recycling. While humankind is magnificently creative, we also turn limited natural resources into materials that will never rot. We daily pollute the land, water, and air, sacrificing the health and beauty of our world.

I used to love walking along any beach I found — the finely-grained canvas repainted with every wave — and seeing man's work returning to nature. There was a strange loveliness and grace in the bow of a boat turning to driftwood, aided by green fingers of moss and the patient trails of snails. Even shards of glass succumbed to the force of waves tumbling them against the shore. I loved how they complemented stones and shells with their own milky, translucent pastels as they journeyed back to being sand. But now, scanning the beach for bits of art and prints of critters, I'm dismayed to find a plethora of plastic instead. What I see there is literally just a drop in the ocean compared with the growing masses in the Pacific, Atlantic, and Caribbean. While some are obnoxiously visible islands of plastic waste, the larger, unseen danger is micro-plastics found in waters worldwide, even in the blood of polar bears.

While I knew enough not to buy lotions or cleansers with micro beads, I only recently realized that microfibers from our synthetic clothes are released with every washing. And just as I was tempted to add some lovely glitter to my holiday cards, I hear that it, too, is made of plastic and is invading our oceans. How sad that plastic, in all its cheap, ubiquitous forms, resists the forces of nature so well, including water, the mother of all cleaners; sand, used for blasting centuries of grime from castles; and dirt, whose microorganisms powerfully break down bones and stones.

I know that many see plastic as a blessing and dirt as a curse. I understand why many people prefer to own things rather than borrow, to buy new rather than used; why they love plastic "disposables" and wouldn't dream of dumpster diving. They don't like dirt. Especially other people's dirt. We've been taught, from our earliest warnings of "Icky! Don't touch!" that cleanliness is next to godliness, or at least it's what keeps us healthy and desirable. Anything less than perfectly clean is an embarrassment and not to be tolerated. But the next time you hear that message, it may be worth your while to consider the source.

You've probably gotten the call. The vacuum cleaner company insists they'll come and clean your carpet for free. All you have to do is watch a short demonstration. I couldn't say no, but I did tell them I was not in a position to buy their machine. "No problem. No pressure," the friendly voice assured me.

The nice young man showed up as promised and began his pitch. He had owned a $600 vacuum, but brought it to the dump when he realized how much better this brand was. *Really?* I had no doubt his product was a good one. But to someone like me, who knew he could have sold or donated the used one, his claim sounded foolish and irresponsible. But I watched the demo with feigned interest. I didn't mind him vacuuming up my dust and cat hair into his demonstration filters—little white circles of purity. I'd never claimed to be an immaculate housekeeper, and he was trained to find the spots I'd missed. But then came his big question. "Are you really comfortable knowing you're sitting on all this dirt?"

I answered honestly. "Actually, one of my favorite places to sit is down on the shore—on the dirt."

"That's different," he insisted. I'm sure he was wishing I had kids—so he could shame me for not protecting their innocent little bottoms from who-knows-what was in those cushions. It was true—there *were* cobwebs in my corners. But it didn't take him long to realize he wasn't going to succeed in embarrassing me into a thousand-dollar purchase. I agree that a clean house *is* a thing of beauty, and a joy to share with guests. If a tool makes cleaning easier, it certainly has value. But surely we can choose our own standard of cleanliness, and what it's worth to us. So I declined the opportunity to buy the salesman's new machine. I trusted that my friends would forgive me for my trespassing dust bunnies, as I forgive theirs.

Resisting an occasional vacuum cleaner salesman is easy. It's more difficult to navigate the seemingly endless proliferation of cleaning products. There are thousands on the market to choose from — a special one for every purpose — and we have antibacterial this and that and disinfectants in every scent and color. Of course, if all these products fail to get your clothes, furniture, or carpet clean, you have a great excuse to throw them away and buy new ones. You get to go shopping, the merchant is happy, the investors get their shares, the government gets its tax, the garbage hauler has work, and everyone wins, right? Maybe — if you believe in the endlessness of natural resources, have a bottomless wallet, are sure climate change is a hoax, and somebody else will figure out what to do about pollution. The magnitude of serious problems generated by waste is borne out by statistics, as well as the evidence I see again and again on the curb.

When I rescued some large sturdy shelves from a topless basement — the house had been moved — I was anxious to reorganize everything in *my* basement, but I waited until spring and kept an eye out for some discarded plastic bins and drawers. Even while passing up the many that were cracked or broken, I picked up a dozen bins and four sets of drawers. Some were dirty, others clean and just a convenient container for their unwanted contents — often a bevy of plastic toys. When did the line between disposables and good, sturdy plastic become so blurred? Cardboard boxes are still available behind many stores, and the multitude of bags we get when buying other things are great for trash. My favorite sturdy "garbage" bags once held water softener salt, kitty litter, cat food, or birdseed. If we really don't need that heavy plastic bin, why not donate it and save that much oil and landfill space? Because it's dirty and we don't want to touch it? Better to use some of those many cleaning products than to dirty up our world with more plastic that will never break down into good old dirt. Am I exaggerating? Well, since it takes 500 to a thousand years for *plastic bags* to disintegrate, I don't think so. When we throw something away, *where is away?*

In 1798, Samuel Coleridge published *The Rime of the Ancient Mariner,* in which the mariner kills an albatross and subsequently suffers devastating weather and the gradual death of his crew. They had hung the body of the bird around the mariner's neck as a reminder of his thoughtless and cruel deed. Hence, the albatross hanging from one's neck has come to symbolize a curse brought upon oneself.

More than 200 years later, Midway Island, in the middle of the Pacific Ocean, was scattered with dead albatross chicks. You may have seen the heartbreaking pictures of bird corpses, with their magnificent beaks and colossal wings (adults can have eight-foot wingspans) decomposing around colorful bottle caps and the deadly plastic potpourri that filled their bellies and left no room for food.

As of May 2018, a sixty-seven-year-old mother albatross has returned to Midway and is raising her newest chick. Tagged in 1956 at the estimated age of five, she is the oldest known wild bird, named Wisdom by the scientists observing her life. Though

What do you suppose Wisdom, the 67-year-old albatross (the oldest known bird in the world) tells her chick? (photo by Dan Clark, U.S. Fish and Wildlife Service)

The unaltered stomach contents of a dead albatross chick photographed on Midway Atoll National Wildlife Refuge in the Pacific in September 2009 include plastic marine debris fed to the chick by its parents. (photo by Chris Jordan licensed through Creative Commons)

nineteen of twenty-one albatross species are endangered, Wisdom has persevered, dancing with her mate and surviving tsunamis. But will her progeny survive our discarded plastic? When I wondered if anyone was still reading the mariner's cautionary tale, I found there are comics and even video games based on the poem. When I discovered that Wisdom had her own Facebook page with 1,474 friends, I couldn't wait to friend her! Her last chick's name is Kukini, meaning Messenger. I hope this means that a generation of young people will heed the warning, embrace *Wisdom* and her *Messenger,* and act to preserve her magnificent species and so many others threatened by our thoughtless consumption and packaging.

If we have any hope of curtailing the plastic Leviathan, we need to stop worshiping convenience and "newness" and get over our embarrassment at reusing things. My millionaire friend, Donna, set a great example. At one of her gatherings in her lovely country kitchen, she used the liner bag from an empty cereal box to send leftovers home with a lucky guest. I'd never thought of that, but why not? I once heard Cool Whip containers referred to as "Credit River Tupperware." Credit River Township, named back when fur traders knew they could get credit there, has one of the highest average income levels in Minnesota. Is the frugal reuse of disposables an anomaly, or a step on the road to riches, or at least being credit worthy?

Let me be clean . . . I mean clear. It's not that I don't believe in germ theory. My dad died of a drug-resistant infection. Perhaps better care early on would have saved his life. But these most deadly bacteria are not simply the result of "dirt." Rather you could say, they're the result of too much cleanliness. The overuse of cleaning agents and antibiotics causes "bugs" to evolve

Could this be why I'm healthy?

into "superbugs." Ironically, aggressively marketed antimicro-
bial soaps have proven to have no measurable health benefits,
because few people wash their hands long enough to let them
work. Yet they go down our drains into our water, polluting
the environment for decades and promoting drug resistance
in human pathogens—the *really* bad germs.

One of my favorite pictures shows me in diapers, a necklace
of clover (*real* clover—not plastic!), eating dirt with a spoon.
My big brother squats nearby with hands digging, his muddy
lips smiling and his raccoon-ringed eyes mischievously planning
his next move, I'm sure.

A few years later I became fascinated by the massive holes
dug in the earth for house foundations. I loved watching the
cliff swallows burrowing into the sandy brown, gray, and golden
striations for their cozy nests. I remember a day spent playing

on what was to me an adventurous Everest of dirt. I came home exhausted, happy, and filthy. Mom looked at my blackened face and said, "Get in the bathtub! And don't play in that dirt again!"

"But, Mom," I protested, "it's clean dirt!"

An oxymoron? Perhaps not. Dr. Vandana Shiva, world-renowned physicist, activist, and expert on quantum theory, speaks fondly of her childhood in India, where they plastered their floors daily with a mixture of soil and dung, a natural antiseptic. She said, "That freedom to play with dirt, I think, has been my intellectual, emotional, and physical immunity builder." She suggests that we treat soil as our sacred mother. If that sounds primitive or New Agey, consider the lesson of the dust bowl. We are still seeing the devastation of dirt caused by industrial farming, monocultures, and strip mining. We have lost a third of our precious topsoil in the last 100 years.

Perhaps on some instinctive level, children know there are many kinds of dirt—and even germs. While adults tend to see them all as dangerous, the truth is, most germs are beneficial. Without them, you'd be dead in two weeks.

Where did I read that? In a fascinating *Psychology Today* article called "The Cult of Clean." It also said that researchers suspect our growing rates of asthma and allergies may be due to insufficient exposure to dirt and microorganisms. By growing up outside, unafraid of dirt, I probably developed all kinds of immunities that keep me healthy. So many people live essentially indoors, in relatively sterile environments. Experts theorize that they lack valuable protections, and that their immune systems, with nothing to fight off, become hyper-sensitive, creating allergies or other autoimmune conditions. Even depression and anxiety may be set off by inflammatory processes, which are worsened by lack of contact with benign microorganisms—clean dirt.

Our obsession with extreme cleanliness may be rooted in peer pressure, in the anonymous but ubiquitous eyes with which advertisers seem to peek into our windows. But experts also say cleaning, like shopping, is simply a favored American response to anxiety. Both responses might seem harmless, but neither really works. Just like overeating, smoking, or drinking, these can be temporary distractions that do little or nothing to change the stressors and often make them worse in the long run.

I do understand colds and flu, and I wash my hands—a lot. But we need to be able to distinguish between a reasonable caution and a paranoia that benefits only the soap industry. Unfortunately, many such products are also filled with toxic chemicals. Though I do use some cleaners, I like recipes using cheap and natural alternatives. I have long preferred using microfiber cloths. They do a fine job, even removing bacteria without the use of smelly soaps or chemicals. But now that I read of microfibers in our water, I'm reconsidering. It seems there are trade-offs in everything.

The sad fact is, as people spend more and more time inside, our indoor air has become more polluted than what's outdoors. Multitudes of cleaning products, dry-cleaning chemicals that remain on clothes, new products off-gassing unknown poisons, and hundreds of varieties of air fresheners fill our homes and our lungs. I always wash my secondhand finds, but sometimes it's more to remove the scent of soap or perfume than for fear of cooties. I've found the best cure for questionable rugs is to leave them outside, thrown over a bench or railing, for the rain to cleanse and the sun to sweeten. (Did you know the Red Cross recommends sunshine to sterilize bandages?) Though I know many people will use a spray to get that "new car scent," I'm grateful that my older finds have long since *lost* their chemical smells.

We are not ignorant or thoughtless people. I admire (and envy!) my friends who have a real gift for cleaning. But we need to unlearn some of what we've been taught to believe. I thanked my mother when she gave me a new plastic cutting board to replace my wooden one. She'd heard it was more sanitary. That made sense to me—until I read of a study proving wood cutting boards were safer, due to wood's natural antiseptic properties. Who knew? If the people making the plastic boards did, they certainly weren't telling. After all, everyone has a wooden cutting board. To hawk their plastic replacements, the corporations needed a believable-sounding reason—whether or not it happened to be true.

So let us be clean, and enjoy our cleanliness. But let us not trade our sanity for being sanitary. Dirt is not evil, and "used" is not a dirty word. Even more importantly, don't let the fear of getting dirty keep you or your children indoors. For outside, the dirt is not only waiting to gift us with immunities. It's also busy growing our food, filtering our waters, and urging the roses to open their pristine beauty to us.

12

The Boat to Heaven

I think every salvager has a bit of archaeologist in her. Almost anything she finds will raise a question or two. Who owned this? Why did she buy this? Was this a gift? What was this used for? How old is this? Why are they getting rid of this?

That last question came to mind when I found a large beautiful granite landscaping stone with the note, "32 more—you haul, you have." Excited, I ran up to the house and asked, "Do you really have thirty-three of these you don't want?"

"Yes, but you'll never be able to lift them."

"Yes, I will."

"They weigh eighty pounds each."

"I know. I lifted the one on the curb."

My little station wagon couldn't handle all that weight at once, so the owner graciously agreed to give me a week to get the one-ton stack out of her backyard.

After completing the heavy but happy task (with friend Allen's gracious help) I went to thank my benefactor again. That's when she pointed out the ring of "stones" circling the tree in the front yard. They were similar in size and shape to what

The clouds no longer looked like an angel by the time I swam back to shore and took the picture, but the sky was still beautiful.

I'd just taken, but made of beige concrete. She said they had replaced the granite ones with these because they matched the house better. *Hmm.* "Besides," she added almost in a whisper, "do you know where the others came from? A company that makes headstones."

There it was, the real reason she'd gone to the trouble and expense to replace genuine granite stones with cement: they made her think of death. Even encircling a garden, these lovely stones seemed, to her, tainted. With what? Disease? Decay? Sadness? (I wonder what she'd think if she heard Julia Child saying she kept her pie crust dough cold by using a piece of marble she found in a graveyard.)

As I planned how I'd use the stones for handsomely sturdy steps around the yard, I thought of how often our memories and associations color our views of the world. I know that some people look at my little log outhouse with amazement, if not disgust. But to me, it brings happy memories of my childhood days at camp, and more. With two windows letting in the woodland breeze, the rarely-used and quickly-emptied chamber pot doesn't smell, any more than did my very favorite outhouse. That one stood atop a mountain in Colorado, remote enough not to need the two walls that were missing. Rain-washed and sun-drenched, it smelled only of mountain air. Mother Nature's watercolor brush had exquisitely stained the brown paper bags lining the remaining walls. A spider had spun her delicate art across the stunning mountain view. Who knew an outhouse could be so majestic—an honest-to-goodness throne!

When Mom found an old picture of me as a toddler sitting in the outhouse on Grandpa Olsen's Iowa farm, I knew my comfortable association had started then. The sun streamed in the open door to light up my little legs dangling and the smile on my face. Trips to summer camps and friends' cabins made other outhouse memories nothing but pleasant, in spite of all

Outhouses probably are not a fond memory for people with no indoor plumbing. But for me, it meant being on Grandpa Olsen's farm, and later at camps or friends' cabins.

the stories of outhouse tippings and jokes about two-storied privies. I still remember a moonlit trip to the potty in the woods where I saw my first luna moth, its graceful four-inch pale-green wings and feathery antennae more magical than Tinkerbell.

Each death is as personal and unique as it is universal. I dare not judge how any person deals with this most intimate experience. But by contemplating death and sharing our experiences with each other, we may be able to soften the blow and enrich the lessons we take away.

My father's death was both a loss and a blessing. His brain had been damaged following an operation. Overnight this strong, smart man lost most of his mental capacity and all recognition of loved ones. We were grateful when he surpassed his prognosis by making a remarkable physical recovery. Our stubborn dad even gained a new sweetness and humility as he learned to accept his limitations. Still, we watched with breaking hearts for ten years as he slipped further and further away. When a foot wound became infected with MRSA (methicillin-resistant staphylococcus aureus) and the doctor started talking about amputation, it was clear that letting the infection be his angel of death would be kinder than taking extraordinary and painful measures he would not be able to understand nor appreciate. The staff agreed it was time for hospice care.

I was told to come that night because he might not make it to morning. I came, stayed the night, another night, and two more, before deciding I'd have to sleep at home and come during the day. Each morning, the nurses were surprised to see him still alive. Six days, eight days, eleven days. With no medication, food, or water, and the hospice workers noting all the signs of death, each shift ended with a farewell, to be followed the next day by a disbelieving hello.

Twelve, thirteen days. The pastor had been in and anointed him. We had all said our goodbyes. The nurses, and my brother and sister and I were seriously worried about Mom's exhaustion. Friends shared caring advice:

"Some people won't die unless you leave them alone." We tried that.

"Make sure everyone's there together." We did.

"Tell him it's okay to go." So Mom told Dad, the lifelong aviator, "You're cleared for takeoff. The runway's yours. I'll be on the next flight."

"Not the *next* flight, Mom! A later one!" I protested.

Fifteen days. My nephew Jeremiah, a world-class athlete, wondered aloud, "We know my heart is exceptionally strong, and that my body has an extraordinary ability to fast and stay hydrated. Maybe I got all that from Grandpa. Maybe that's what's keeping him alive."

When my boss called to check on me and I shared that with her, she said, "Maybe you should donate his body to science."

The morning of the sixteenth day, I called Mom and asked what she thought. "Yes—that's what he would want." I agreed, knowing Dad loved science and hated wasting things. It was Saturday, and I doubted I could make any arrangements, but I told her I'd try. I found University of Minnesota—Body Bequest Program in the phone book and called.

"Sure, we'd be very grateful to take the body for study."

They faxed the forms to the nursing home, where Mom signed them and faxed them back. She kissed Dad goodbye, *again,* and went home. She called to tell me she felt an incredible sense of peace. She was so sure that signing that paper made Dad happy. Within an hour her phone rang. He had finally taken off.

Coincidence? Perhaps. But we cried with relief and smiled, wondering why we hadn't thought of donation earlier. It seemed perfectly natural that Dad would want to be recycled and make one more contribution to society.

With the body gone on to its next purpose, we concentrated on making our celebration of his life also fit what he would have wanted. I wondered if I should go buy a dress. A *new* dress. That's what people do for funerals, right? Hating shopping as I did, and beyond exhausted, I stopped at the senior center rummage sale. There I found a perfect dress. Brand new, my size, a cheerful yet respectful black-and-white floral print. Three dollars. Was it okay to wear a rummage sale dress to Dad's service? He would say yes; so I did.

After that I thought I really should order a nice flower arrangement. It was too early to create one from the garden, since nothing was blooming yet. But then I thought about Dad, who'd never cared much about flowers. When Mom ran across a small wooden airplane in his things, it reminded me that his favorite perspective on life was always from the sky. I envisioned what he saw as he happily flew over the lake behind their house.

I searched my garage and found a large, sturdy old basket. I lined it with mosses gathered from the woods and baby plants I found in the nurseries. My sister, Nancy, joined me excitedly to recreate the patchwork landscape of farm fields we'd seen so many times from Dad's plane. Tiny stones became boulders and petite sweet alyssum grew into Lilliputian lilac bushes. Dried sprigs took the role of ancient trees. A borrowed miniature house was

The "flowers" at Dad's celebration of life truly celebrated him and his love of flying.

perfect next to the broken mirror and scrap of blue cellophane that became the lake, complete with toothpick dock. The finishing touch was the model airplane in the cotton clouds suspended over the scene. It cost about the same as an arrangement would have and took a lot of time, but it connected us with Dad in a creative and healing way. We were happy to be able to share that connection with everyone who came to his service. Our home-made arrangement was beautiful, and more unique and personal than anything we could have bought. It was all about Dad.

Even more "Dad" was the white dove my neighbor brought to the service. Perched in its white cage on the baptismal font, it provided a focal point for the service, since we had neither body nor ashes. How much cheerier it was to have that living symbol, not only of the Spirit, but also of Dad and his love of flight! As the service ended, we all went outside to the fresh May sunshine and stood in a circle while Marsha brought her dove—for this moment, our dove—around for each of us to touch and say our farewells. Then my niece Kym had the honor of releasing it. Watching it soar into the clear-blue sky, it was easy to see Dad taking off and feeling the joy of his hard-won freedom. It was also, for us, more joyful than it would have been to watch him being lowered into the ground.

I wouldn't criticize anyone for how they decide to honor and

Thanks to Donna Green for capturing this special moment, Dad's take-off, while I held back tears. I wasn't sad, just deeply moved, as his death was certainly a sweet release.

send off their loved ones. Seeing the exquisitely handcrafted coffin my cousin Tammy and her husband made for her mother took my breath away and brought tears to my eyes, though it didn't make me want one for my parents or myself. Acts of love come in many forms.

On the other hand, when I read about the enormous cost of a typical American funeral, and the hard-sell tactics sometimes used to manipulate the bereaved into paying for it, what echoes in my mind is Led Zeppelin's song about the lady who thinks she can buy a "Stairway to Heaven." It pleases me to see that simpler, more affordable, and greener ways of dealing with death are becoming more available and acceptable.

I don't know where that Stairway to Heaven is, but the Boat to Heaven is in my backyard.

There in the shady woods, formed by the skeleton of a tree stump and draped in fragrant moss lies a three-foot phantom vessel. In the center stands the mast—a young aspen tree, its green and gold leaves catching the breeze like little sails.

When you live in the woods, you see things die. Birds fly into my windows, my cats dutifully catch rodents, an occasional squirrel or rabbit meets its death by drowning. Always saddened by these innocent deaths, I began to put these creatures in that velvety, peaceful place that looked so much like a boat that might rock one gently to sleep. The critter's body is always gone by morning, so it must truly be the Boat to Heaven. Knowing that each furry or feathered little thing has given life to some owl or coyote or other pallbearer of the night gives me great peace. All is as it should be in the circle of life.

Not too far from the Boat to Heaven is my favorite nurse log. In life, this tree towered over the lake and hosted countless generations of birds. In death, it rests on the shore, soaking up water and sun; giving life to thousands of organisms, plants, and tiny critters that grow in and on its maternal breast. In return, they break it down into the precious topsoil we depend upon for the food we eat every day. (Maybe if we spend a little more time in the forest, witnessing the lush communities of life springing from dying plants, we'll be more inclined to compost our food scraps, rather than putting them into a garbage disposal where they are headed for our waters.)

Careful observation can illuminate many aspects of life and death, but the ultimate mystery remains. Mom's great peace at our decision to donate Dad's body remained with her, and she gave us clear instructions to do the same for her. As she aged

People seem to prefer to burn or chip logs these days, rather than let them lie and nurse communities of new life. Reno and I loved this nurse log for many years.

in body and mind, we spoke of the Native American belief that when an eagle flies overhead, it blesses you. Mom had long been ready to fly off as an angel and excitedly told me she'd drop me a feather and a blessing. So when she finally made it out of here in the spring of 2017, friends started asking me, "Has she dropped you a feather yet?"

You probably know by now that Nature is my Other Mother. So I wasn't too surprised when, after Mom's celebration of life, I came home to find friends greeting me as I swam in my lake. Two grand birds soaring high—eagles or vultures? Either would be symbolic, as both eat carrion, turning the dead into new energy. A white dove, just like the one we released ten years earlier at Dad's celebration, circled over me. Dad? Is that you? Or Mom, going to join Dad? Or (smile) just one of the many white doves my neighbors John and Marsha released at another event that day, returning home to roost? I didn't care if it was spirit or symbol—it made me cry happy tears. Then swallows, catching the sun on their golden breasts as they swooped, and a perfect row of sixteen geese flying overhead with that wonderful sound of swishing wings. But best of all, as I reached the middle of our little lake, was a great blue heron that dipped gracefully over me with its six-foot wingspan.

Each beautiful bird was a generous blessing. Then who shows up but the goose family that had been visiting me daily. So I called to them, and they followed me to the dock for a little picnic of corn: the perfect closing to the long vigil with Mom and the busy weeks of preparation for the day of her celebration. I finally relaxed.

A week later Father Goose showed up with one of his wing feathers askew, time to molt and grow new ones for the

I knew it was highly unlikely that Father Goose would drop that feather where I might find it . . .

migration. I told him it would be nice if he dropped it here for me, but I felt silly, knowing that was pretty unlikely. The family traveled a wide range over this lake and the next. But I did take a good look at it, just in case, and noticed a distinct stain on one side and a split on the other.

The next day I went down to the dock for my swim, not thinking about the geese or the feather. But there it was. *The* feather. I was astonished, but it was unmistakable. It looked not at all dropped, but as if it had been carefully, artfully, deliberately placed there. I imagined Mom smiling as I kissed it, then dove in for my swim.

I couldn't take my eyes off the beautiful sky—another shining contrail heading up to heaven, golden clouds in the west, and deep-blue ones in the east that morphed into—an angel! A broad skirt, two outstretched wings, a round head crowned with a halo turning gold. Of course the clouds had drifted by the time I got back to shore and took pictures, but they were

. . . but there it was, where I couldn't help but find it, with the same definite stain and split.

Watching this pair of loons as they danced and flirted for hours was my meditation.

still beautiful. I brought the feather in and looked forward to telling people about it and the angel. But did I really believe they were sent by Mom?

Two months after that extraordinary day, the feather still lay on my table, but the geese were gone. Their strong new feathers

Every night I would chat with this tree frog in my window. His pose, serenity, slight smile, and round belly made me think of the Buddha.

My mother had gotten her wish and gone on, but there were loving mothers all around me.

had carried them into the sky, where they joined other families preparing to migrate. I missed them, and Mom. But then a pair of loons came and flirted, danced, and hooted for hours while I took their pictures from my canoe.

A doe stood on the shore, nursing her fawn, and soothing my heart. My friendly sunfish Greenie finally left the nest he'd been cleaning and guarding so long. I hoped he avoided the hooks and would return for a third summer with me. But then I had a new green friend—a tree frog. He sat on my kitchen window every night, as calm as a little Buddha even with the clatter of dishes and my chattering to him.

Could any of these really have been signs from Mom? I don't know. But it doesn't really matter. They brought me great joy and comfort as they reminded me daily of the constant change that is life. One season after another. Life inevitably moving on to death to make room for the next joyful birth.

13
Totem Pole
Mystery and History

A Friday night and my car was full of trashy treasures salvaged from the curbside pickup piles. Time to go home. But I pulled into one last cul-de-sac and found a tall slender . . . *something* . . . standing there on the road. Getting out, I was greeted by, "Want a totem pole?"

I could barely see the man who asked, or the totem pole, but I replied, "Yes. Yes, I do."

Then, as with any find, I thought twice about whether I really wanted it, where I'd put it, and what I'd do with it. As my eyes adjusted to the dark, I saw that the pole was in pretty bad shape, but there was no question it would fit in with my rustic yard. The bottom figure — a man or a bear? — holding the fish would look perfect by the lake. And the eagle, even in its woodpecker-ravaged and decomposing state, with broken beak, still had some of the majesty that all eagles seem to have. The man who had spoken showed me the wings and tail, long since rotted off the body. Could I find a way to reattach them?

But there's another question: is it right for me to take this? I remembered being out with a Native American friend when we drove past a hotel flaunting a totem pole. She said she hated it when places used "Indian décor" for commercial gain. I agreed.

I'd been to lectures where American Indian scholars explained why, to many, the use of Indian caricatures by sports teams and others seemed only to add to the insensitivity toward their people. I understood. But this was different, wasn't it? Art was often an important bridge between cultures. Could this totem pole serve that purpose if I brought it home to my yard?

I asked the man if it might be authentic. He didn't know but thought it probably was, since the house had been full of artifacts when he bought it from "an old Jewish cowboy with an Indian girlfriend." *Hmm.* More curiosity, few answers. But I knew if I didn't rescue this, it'd be crushed by the jaws of a garbage truck in a few hours. The majestic icon seemed as lost and injured as a puppy on the side of the road. I just had to pick it up. I needed time to figure out what it was and what should be done with it.

The next morning, my neighbors helped me carry my heavy, ten-foot find from the car and set it up by my little cabin out back. Less than two hours later, a bald eagle flew slowly over it. *Thanks for blessing it,* I thought with a smile. I wondered if an elder had blessed it when it was made, as was the tradition. Examination in the midday sun convinced me the pole was carved with a chainsaw. The notion that it may have been made by some white guy at a county fair dispelled some of the mystique, but also carried a sense of relief. *It's probably not some ancient sacred treasure. But it is old, fascinating, and uniquely beautiful.* A closer look at both ends revealed a lot of rot and an active colony of carpenter ants. *Restoring it will be more challenging than I expected. But it's too late. I've already begun to bond with it.*

The course of my summer was set—reading books on totem

poles and checking the internet, home stores, and friends for ideas on how to restore a largely rotted, grayed, and cracked piece of wood. I got advice varying from "give up—it's a goner" to "cut the eagle off and hire someone to carve a new one." I considered it all and settled on a plan—one which evolved into thirty steps and required the help of generous neighbors. (See "How We Renovated My Totem Pole" in the back of this book.) The process took all summer, but I was happy, recreating the original, yet making it my own. I softened the angles to make it a bit more realistic and strove to rebuild a powerful yet friendly beak. The bright-yellow eyes I'd saved from a long-gone plastic owl, along with some careful painting, gave it the perfect expression—all-seeing but not quite menacing. A mixture of stains covered the weathered gray with a rich, protective brown.

My research taught me that our local woodland and prairie tribes never made totem poles. That made sense, since they required large cedar trees *and* coastal waters for transport. The Pacific Northwest Coast tribes are best known for this art form, but people of New Zealand, Japan, and Africa also made poles. The bear, fish, and eagle were common motifs, though the hand-carved work of the coastal peoples looked more graceful and artistically stylized than mine.

Some early Christians believed that totem poles were worshiped or used to ward off evil spirits. I knew those were myths but wondered if my neighbor John's deep Christian faith might make him hesitant to help me. But no. Besides being one of those guys who can fix *anything,* he is also a wise and generous elder. He became the eagle's best friend. Standing on a ladder, he poured cup after cup of the polyether foam I mixed into the bandaged eagle and patiently watched the mixture expand to replace the rotted interior wood. Once it hardened, I cringed as he drilled a long metal rod through my bird! But his surgical instincts proved true, and the rod became the bone that reattached both wings. *Whew.* When I read that some ancient poles were as practical as house pillars or mortuary poles, which are built with a sort of "casket" on top, I wondered if they sometimes needed reinforcement too.

Some poles have special meanings, such as memorial poles or shame poles. (I hear there's a shame pole in Alaska depicting former Exxon CEO, Lee Raymond, whose company failed to finish cleaning up the oil spilled in the Exxon-Valdez disaster or pay the court-ordered damages.) Then there are welcoming poles—often a naked man—*hmm!* Why naked? The books didn't say. But whether serious or whimsical, the designs most often told of the owner's clan and accomplishments, of life events, or of folk stories and songs. Overall, they came to symbolize the belief that the forces of nature are our spiritual brethren—that certainly fits in my yard and life.

When I read that a totem pole is like a coat of arms saying, "This is who I am," I wanted to know even more about mine. Since it didn't have a bear's ears, I suspected the figure holding the fish was a man. My favorite interpretation of why the tongue sticks out is that the creature is conveying knowledge or power. I decided to stand in front of him more often! The eagle, because it's the bird that flies highest and closest to the Creator, represents the Great Spirit. What better symbol to have outside my highest window, keeping one eye on the precious lake and land and the other looking in on me.

I was learning a lot, but I still wondered if the ownership of a totem pole by a non-native person might offend indigenous people. The last thing I wanted was for this artifact—whatever its origin—to cause insult or resentment. I asked a couple of Native American friends if my having this totem pole offended them, and they said no, because it wasn't a tradition of their tribe. But how would those who created the original poles feel?

I've heard it suggested that interest in another's culture is due

Braids and canoes fit in several cultures. I loved taking my niece, Angela, canoeing when she was a kid, and it's time for us to go again.

to a lack of knowledge of one's own roots. But I think my interest began with the respect my dad expressed when he introduced us kids to his American Indian friend, who generously showed us his beautiful headdress and taught my brother to hunt. As I grew, the deeper attraction was this: Indian culture and spirituality, more than my own, seemed rooted in connections to the earth and animals, where I found so much of my personal peace and joy.

I had been enthralled by the story of Heidi. But her life in the mountains, playing among the goats and sleeping in her grandfather's hayloft, is the only earthy European role model I remember. When I grew out my hair and wore it in long braids like hers, people seemed to identify them as Indian more often than Alpine, despite their pale color. Maybe that's because there are more Native Americans than mountains in Minnesota.

I had the privilege of working at Indian Upward Bound one summer, where I learned to do this beadwork.

Culture is geographical as well as genetic. Coming of age in the sixties, we strove to leave the suburban, white-washed fifties behind and get back to the earth. That meant there was cross-over between hippie and traditional Indian style, both deliberate and accidental. All of this drew me to a *wacipi* (powwow) at Bdote Minisota—the sacred confluence of the Minnesota and Mississippi Rivers, where I joined in the dance and found a quiet place in the woods to curl up in my sleeping bag under the stars. There I discovered that, like the blues and gospel I'd come to love, Indian art and music touched a place in my soul, even though I could never sing in that style. The drums at wacipis or ceremonies still move me.

I decided to dig more deeply and spent a summer as a camp counselor at Indian Upward Bound, learning Ojibwe language, history, and arts with urban Native teenagers. Though immersed in the community, I knew I would not fully understand or be a part of certain things. I respected their request that I not attend the classes on spirituality. I only remember a few words of Ojibwe, but the history class taught me things I can't forget. Hearing of children taken from their families and placed in boarding schools is one thing. Knowing that some of the elders you are living with may have suffered the "acculturation" of being stripped of their clothing, hair, language, and names is something else. Emotional, physical, and sexual abuse was rarely spoken of, but not because it didn't happen.

As I got to know the kids and staff as individuals, it was clear that an idealized, romanticized vision of Native American life was no more accurate than the movies of savages fighting cowboys in white hats. I was shocked when I once found some boys tearing the legs from a frog. Weren't *all* Indians supposed to naturally love and respect animals? They were just as surprised to see me excitedly pick up a lime-green caterpillar as fat as my thumb. These city kids didn't know the "creepy-crawly" thing I gently held would magically morph into a spectacular cecropia moth, with huge, velvety, red-and-brown wings. So we learned from each other.

I deeply appreciated that experience and later shared what I learned by teaching classes to suburban kids. My students learned to do bead work and speak a few Ojibwe words while they also received an eye-opening introduction to certain dark chapters of the white-man's history rarely mentioned in their textbooks. I hoped if more people knew about the hundreds

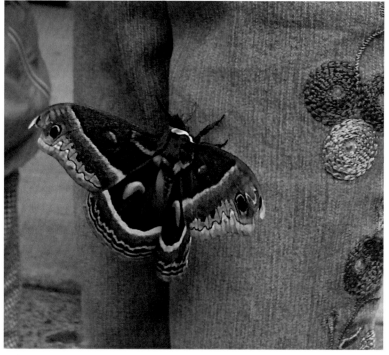

A fat green caterpillar looks different once you know it's the beginning of a gorgeous cecropia moth.

of broken treaties and imagined the damage done to children being taken from their parents, we might not let it happen again.

Years later, when my focus on music meant spending more time in nightclubs and less time in the woods, I took an acting class, hoping it would make me more comfortable on stage. When instructed to pick an object to focus on, to close my eyes and open my heart, I touched the small antique Indian ring on my little finger. I rarely bought jewelry, but I'd loved the pale turquoise stone with golden-brown veins from the moment I saw it. I always wore it, so I was surprised when my tears came quickly. I didn't recognize the Indian elder who appeared to me, nor did I hear him speak, but his message was clear. He was calling me back to the forest. My soul needed to keep one foot in the natural world in order to feel stable and alive.

Decades later, I felt true to the elder who had appeared behind my closed eyes and more grounded in the forest than ever. But here I was — still feeling ignorant about this totem pole but determined to do it justice. I learned that the original carvers would have left a rotting pole to fall and return to the earth, then make a new one. I knew I couldn't do that! I wished I could have renovated the pole with just natural materials, not the plastic expanding foam it required. Then I remembered reading that totem poles increased in number and quality when white traders introduced iron tools that replaced the stones, shells, and beaver teeth originally used for carving. Now carvers save time and effort by using chainsaws for the first rough cuts on their poles. Rather than lament the onset of new technology, they appreciate its advantages, just as Woodland Indians embraced glass beads brought by European traders. They replaced porcupine quills with the more colorful and lasting beads, creating an incredible new art form. Native American art museums show more and more innovative expressions of traditional arts.

When I failed in my efforts to find the origin of my totem pole, I began to simply accept it as a cultural bridge. Even those who chuckled when they first heard, "Holly has a totem pole!" stood before it and said, "Wow."

The tribes who made totem poles always raised them with a ceremonial potlatch. When I finally finished my summer of work on the pole, I opted for just a dinner thanking all the neighbors who helped me recreate it, but shared some of the history I'd learned. From the 1890s to the 1950s, the white man's religious paranoia outlawed the potlatch, virtually stopping the creation of the poles. Ironically, it was also the white man who preserved many poles in museums while those left out in the elements rotted. Only recently, encouraged by the Native American Graves Protection and Repatriation Act, have some been returned to their rightful owners.

My totem pole continues to stand against the weather, though it's due for some more protective work from me. It's probably my favorite piece of art. But I'm also grateful for the journey of learning it inspired. Documentaries, books, interviews, and lectures remind me that life for indigenous people on reservations and in urban areas is improving, but still fraught with tragedies and challenges. Attending wacipis reminds me that laughter and joy and family bonds also persist, buoyed up by the bright tinkling sound of jingle-dress dances and swirling colors of fringed shawls. Traditions and languages are being revived. I've come to recognize the scents of sweet grass and sage that bring healing in times of celebration or grief. When I hear anyone demonize the unfamiliar, I'm even more grateful

Rain drove the 2016 Shakopee Mdewankanton Sioux Wacipi indoors, but didn't dampen the spirits of the dancers.

for the Native scholars, writers, artists, and humorists who open doors of understanding by telling ancient stories and new ones.

While the eagle atop my totem pole watches over me, I am also reminded that the survival of land and people go hand in hand—from the slaughter of bison, the spilling of oil, the destruction of wilderness, to the rise of sea level and devastating storms. I am happy to see new cross-cultural alliances being formed to protect the earth—mother to all beings and cultures.

To hear the music of another's voice, to see the design woven by the hours of another's life, to sense the fragility and strength of that silver cord with which every man, woman, and child is singularly holding to his or her divine spirit, is to begin to feel

The majestic bison and the cultures of Indigenous Peoples neared extinction, but both are coming back strong.

empathy — the empathy we need in order to know that every person, every frog and creepy crawly thing is not just being, but is *becoming* and is precious in the circle of life — the empathy to heal the wounds we have suffered and those we have inflicted, and to let go of the battle, unbeaten and ready to grow together.

My friend Mary Roon, on Washington State's Olympic Peninsula, kindly put me in touch with Dale Faulstich, a master carver respectfully endorsed and hired by the nearby tribe to carve three enormous poles. He is non-Native. There was the simple answer to my complicated question. The skill, respect, and heart of a man are what matters — not the color. In our correspondence, he agreed that art belongs to all humanity. He also confirmed my suspicion that my pole, though nicely done, was made by a hobbyist, and that the bottom figure was a man, not a bear.

14
Reaping the Harvest of the Blues

Knowing how I wrestled with questions of cultural appropriation when I found my totem pole, you might wonder if I had the same questions when I began to sing the blues. I probably would have if not for my incredible luck early on.

I was enthralled by the blues the first time I heard that music live. I had the strange sensation that it was coming out of me at the same time it entered my ears, even though I didn't know anything about it. I thought my new friend Tony was crazy when he introduced me to Willie Dixon and said, "Holly doesn't know it yet, but she sings." Willie Dixon (1915–1992), was arguably the most highly respected blues writer of his time, and an important link between the blues and rock and roll. He wrote hundreds of songs, some of which were recorded and performed by Chuck Berry, Grateful Dead, The Doors, and The Rolling Stones, among others. Why would Tony tell this master that I sing?

I didn't, but could I? The thought lit a fire in me. I started listening more, learning songs, practicing, and eventually tried out for bands. Willie happened to be in town when I had an

This sharecropper's shack may appeal to those of us who like simplicity and history. But to someone who actually lived in one, perhaps not.

audition and he generously offered to join us. The band could hardly believe it when this legendary black giant with the broad smile and twinkling eyes came and listened to us rehearse in a small basement.

What I remember best is when he said to me, "Don't let anyone tell you that you can't sing the blues because you're white. If you feel it, you should sing it. And I know you feel it."

Who was I to question Willie Dixon?

Tony also introduced me to Taj Mahal, treasured for his blues, folk, and world music. We drove him to a nearby town for his gig, which gave us a chance to chat. Not long after that, I found Koko Taylor, the Queen of the Blues, sitting at a table at the club where she was singing. When I shared that I knew her mentor, Willie Dixon, she generously invited me and my guitar player, Rick, to her home in Chicago. We had a wonderful three days there, whether at Buddy Guy's Checkerboard Lounge where Koko was singing or in her living room where she taught me to sing Willie's "Big Boss Man."

I was surprised and grateful to the music icons who kindly mentored and encouraged me. I wondered what I could do to thank them. Though I knew they were accustomed to fancier surroundings, I thought, just maybe, with their country roots, they would appreciate a change. I told them about my simple log cabin and invited Koko Taylor and her band for dinner, and Taj Mahal and his for lunch. They accepted. Taj said he liked coming to Minnesota because people treated him like a friend rather than an idol, and he proved it by jumping at the chance to fish from my neighbor's little wooden rowboat.

I think these positive relationships with musicians who were down to earth, regardless of their star status, were what enabled

I loved the three days I spent at Koko Taylor's home in 1978. She coached me in her living room as her sweet granddaughter Peaches listened. The snapshot may be faded, but the memory is vivid.

me to meet others with comfort. True, there were a few I didn't care for, but most of the blues folks I met were friendly and genuine. Along with learning and being entertained by their performances night after night, I got to hear their off-stage stories, often as entertaining and enlightening as their music. They were like one big family and treated me as such, encouraging me to get to know the others.

On the top of that list was B.B. King. Everyone called him the best, not only musically, but in personality. Standing in line to meet him backstage at Orchestra Hall in 1978, I saw his patient kindness as fans gushed. So when it was my turn, I told him I didn't want to bother him for an autograph. I would be honored to shake his hand and thank him for his music. That must have been refreshing, because it started a friendship that lasted until his death in 2015.

Mr. King was constantly on the road and overseas, so I was thankful for any time we had to talk. When he was in town and I invited him for dinner, he declined, saying that the words "log cabin" brought memories of cold wind whistling through cracks and rain coming through the roof in his childhood home. Knowing that young Riley lived alone in a sharecropper's shack after his mother and grandmother died, who can blame him for preferring his life on the road in fancy hotels? Yet this humble man never thought less of me for my humble home or my rummage sale clothes.

Mr. King always dressed as a gentleman, not just on stage. I was always careful to dress up for his concerts, and he often complimented me. But one day, just meeting him for a chat, I wore my new blue jeans with smart leather boots and jacket, thinking I looked pretty good. He didn't criticize me, but I could tell he wasn't impressed. That's when he told me why he never wore blue jeans. As a hungry child, sharecropping on his own at age nine, all he had to wear were overalls. Denim reminded him of those hard days.

Yet he never stopped working hard. His tenacity, along with talent and graciousness, lifted him from profound poverty and the oppressive Mississippi culture of the 1920s and '30s into other worlds, where kings and presidents honored him. Even then, there were rough periods when the blues were far from popular and there were pressures to change his style. But no, he insisted on staying true to the blues he loved. Yet I often heard him tell how he adamantly refused and refuted the picture of the laid-back raggedy blues man on the porch with the jug of moonshine by his bare feet. Mr. King persisted, gently tearing down walls and changing much more than his own world. His distinguished image is part of that change, not only an expression of prosperity but also of freedom and dignity.

B.B. King was a true raconteur, sharing wisdom and laughter in his many stories.

B.B., like Willie, Koko, and other prominent blues musicians I was privileged to meet, had always encouraged me as I explored this new world of music. The masters seemed to want to share their art. The adoption of the blues by musicians and fans around the world was what kept their music alive and allowed them to make a living at it. But I also knew African Americans who resented white people for "stealing" their music.

So one day I brought that up while the King of the Blues and I talked about my totem pole. I told him I suspected he and others with deep roots in the blues knew they would always own that musical treasure and asked him what he felt about whites performing it. His eloquent answer: "Just as Native Americans feel that no one owns the land, I believe that no one owns the blues. Music is from the soul, and your soul is not the same as mine, and my soul is not the same as Willie Dixon's, and Willie's is not the same as Robert Johnson's." (Johnson was an even earlier blues master.) "When different people play the blues, it's different, yet the same, like refining oil into gas or churning milk into butter and buttermilk."

I thanked him for the wise and reassuring words.

I never pretended to sing with the depth of those, like B.B. and Koko, who spent years sweating in the cotton fields "from kin to cain't" (from when you kin see to when you cain't). I didn't expect to truly understand what it felt like to be persecuted for the color of my skin, though there were moments when I had a taste. Yet the blues was the art form that fit my voice and soul more deeply than any other music. Why? I don't know. But just as the connection I felt to Native American culture drew me to experience it, my love for the blues compelled me to seek out the masters. And just as I learned more than beadwork at

Indian camp, I learned so much more than music from those who lived the blues and shared their stories.

I had noticed that many of the white friends I liked the most had grown up on farms, and that was also true of my favorite blues players. Even Taj Mahal, who grew up in Massachusetts with musical parents, fell in love with farming at sixteen, becoming a foreman by nineteen and nearly committing to that life. I'm glad he realized he had a lot to give the world through his unique music. But I've always wondered if connection to the earth played a role in my connection to the blues. Then there's also the factor of hard work. I've never worked quite as hard as my blues-playing friends. But as I share in my "marshmallow" chapter, a history of working, going without, and waiting for rewards tends to develop resilience and other positive personality traits—ones that draw my respect and make me want to connect.

I've also been struck by the generosity of some of these artists who grew up in deep poverty—not just sharing of things, time, and money, but the generosity of spirit that can change people. I saw joy in the faces of white men and women as the magic of the blues washed over them. I watched the warmth of the artists who shared their music begin to melt away fear and racism. But the effects of their performances were often bigger than that. Just as a shame pole exposed the wrongs of an oil company, B.B. King's many prison concerts brought in the press and exposed the fact that way too many young black men were being held for extended periods without trials. The blues became a bridge between inmates and lawyers and created the Foundation for Advancement of Inmate Rehabilitation and Recreation.

I deeply appreciated all I experienced and learned from the

many blues masters I met. They convinced me that I could sing, but I knew that I had nothing close to the talent, drive, and passion that I saw in their eyes every day. Seeing the challenges of life on the road and in blues bars, I knew it wasn't for me. There was always that Indian elder's call to come back to the forest.

So I did, and I grew more and more content living a life outdoors and in my rustic little home, working in the library and writing music. I joined a black gospel choir and found that it fit my voice and touched my heart much more than did my childhood Lutheran choir. Whether on Sunday mornings or at one of the many special events where we sang, I got a wider and deeper perspective on America's history and more. We were the "Greek chorus" in the Guthrie Theater's *The Gospel at Colonus*, where the blend of gospel stylings and the story of Oedipus Rex brought the audience (and us) to tears and to our feet. But even more moving were the concerts we did in prisons. Faces that seemed cold, angry, or hurting as they came into the room melted into tears and joy as we sang our hearts out. I'll never forget that experience and the smiles and embraces we all shared after the music.

I loved the experience of singing in that choir, but even more, I treasure the friendships that were born there in the eighties and have endured since. Many of the extraordinary voices that were raised in praise can still be heard on stages near and far, singing in genres from gospel to jazz, soul, pop, classical, and more, and often acting as well. Whether winning Grammys or helping me and others to bid farewell to our loved ones, they always inspire. We all have busy lives (theirs more accomplished than mine!), but I can count on my "sisters by choice" to care, to share, and to bring hearty laughter and hugs to any gathering.

Singing with the Rance Majestic Choir was different from singing the blues, but just as rich an experience.

While I was singing in the choir, recycling everything, crafting words to share my thoughts, and carving out my niche in the woods with my strong, weathered hands, my blues friends lived on custom-made buses and in fancy hotels, telling their stories with soul-stirring voices and making legendary music with their strong, manicured hands. As much as I enjoyed my lifestyle, would I think of criticizing them for not buying used goods or recycling? Of course not. Nor did they ever shame me for my humble garb or unpolished nails. They had good taste, but they also had true class. They understood that from our similar hearts spring differing missions and tools with which to accomplish them. They had been around the world and seen countless ways to honor the arts, the earth, and our fellow beings. They knew that it takes every note in the scale, and a few in between, to fill the air with beautiful music.

We didn't stay in touch as often as we all aged, but I saw these

Koko gave me this around 1993. It shows her glitter and her grit. (photo by Sandro Miller courtesy of Alligator Records)

friends when they were in town and was glad if we had a chance to catch up. The summer of 2009 found me full of tears and precious memories when I traveled to Chicago again, this time for

Koko's funeral. The elegant gold gown and tiara she wore and the many letters of praise were most fitting for someone who had elevated herself from an orphaned child (tossed around "from pillar to post," as she put it the last time we spoke) to a true queen, respected and loved around the world. But what I will remember most are her genuine smile, hearty laugh, and profound love of the music she influenced and preserved.

Many stories Mr. King told me came alive when I traveled to Mississippi for his funeral. I couldn't resist stopping to see the compound-like motel composed of authentic sharecropper shacks near the historic Hopson Plantation. I was intrigued by how they'd added big flat-screen TVs and air conditioning to each shack while preserving its rustic history and flavor. I'm sure I would have enjoyed one of the bluesy events held in the grassy common area. But I doubted that B.B. had ever stopped there, knowing what emotions it might have stirred. It seems the child is father to the man, one way or another. Spending time in the B.B. King Museum and Delta Interpretive Center made that clear. Its mission is similar to Mr. King's lifelong goal: to "empower, unite, and heal through music, art, and education, and share with the world the rich cultural heritage of the Mississippi Delta."

On the way back to Minnesota, I stopped in Memphis to visit the National Civil Rights Museum with a friend. Standing near the balcony of the Lorraine Hotel where Dr. Martin Luther King, Jr. was shot was chilling and brought back the terrible significance of that day. The bus with the statue of Rosa Parks defiantly sitting near the front was more hopeful. But it also reminded me of the story my parents told me about their honeymoon in New Orleans. They boarded a bus and promptly sat in the back.

Club Ebony, "Where the black people go."

Time passed, and they wondered why the bus wasn't moving. Finally the driver came back and told them he could not move the bus until they moved to the front. It was 1945. They were young, just nineteen and twenty-one, and far from home. They knew it was wrong, but what could they do?

It was 2015 and I was sixty-six, but felt I had just found myself in a similar situation. On the eve of Mr. King's funeral, I was excited to go to the Club Ebony, a tiny but historic place where he developed his art. I stood on the corner of Church Street and asked a handsome young black man in a cowboy hat for directions. "It's right down this block. That's where the black people go. The white people go to the Blue Biscuit." I was stunned. I'd often read how B.B. had brought the races together there in his hometown. The young man had grown up there, moved to

Blue Biscuit, "Where the white people go."

Texas, and was back for the special weekend. He was as nice as could be in our brief conversation, but assured me that Indianola was still segregated, except when B.B. was visiting. He asked some passing black women if it would be okay for me to go to the Ebony, and they said sure. But it was late and dark in the small town. I was hungry, tired, alone, and a thousand miles from home. I remembered Mr. King's manager telling me that security around the funeral would be high because there were threats made, as there were throughout his life, even as beloved as he was.

Torn, I went to the Blue Biscuit. The food was good, the music (a white blues band) was great, there were pictures of B.B. and other blues legends on the walls. But I was sad. I hoped the nice man in the cowboy hat was wrong, and that things had changed

191

more than he thought. But I ran into him again the next day, and others I spoke with confirmed what he said. Only white kids could go to the prom, and there were stores where blacks dare not shop. I was tempted to stay another night, hoping there would be a mixed crowd at the Ebony after the funeral. I suspect there was, because of all the visitors in town, but I was too exhausted to go. I hope I'll have another opportunity.

I'll always be grateful that I was able to squeeze into the overflowing church for the service. I'll never again hear "Precious Lord" as I did there, with Mr. King's voice flowing from the speakers above those of the children's choir. As in the best funerals, there were a few funny stories and even jabs at the deceased. He had his flaws, as we all do. His habit of work-ing nearly 365 days a year inevitably left many with frustrations and disappointments. But the three hours of accolades, music, and honors from President Obama, Stevie Wonder, and so many more reminded us all just how extraordinary this man was. He received every award in his field, including the highest possible—the Presidential Medal of Freedom. Yet person after

I made sure I could find the Bell Grove Missionary Baptist Church. The next morning, the church, grounds, and B.B. King Road would be flooded with people mourning and celebrating the King of the Blues.

person spoke of his humility. As one man put it, Mr. King changed the world, but the world never changed him. The next morning, the continental breakfast room at the small hotel where I stayed buzzed with talk about B.B. and the many times he quietly helped people—old friends or strangers—when they needed it.

Driving home, I couldn't help but think how heartbreaking it must have been for B.B. to return to Indianola every year, honoring his hometown and hoping to inspire the children, knowing it would still be segregated when he left.

Though I won't forget what I learned that day, I've chosen to remember him throwing his head back in exuberant laughter, as he so often did; to remember that he never let the pain and discrimination he faced all his life make him bitter; and to remember what Koko said about the blues: "It touches the place that hurts, then heals it."

15

An Old Hippie's Take on Fashion

"Beware of all enterprises that require new clothes."

Henry David Thoreau

My friend Pat recently said, "You're the old hippie we all wish we were." When my eyebrows went up, she smiled and added, "without the sex and drugs."

I don't remember calling myself a hippie back in the day, but now, occasionally seeing my teenage friends wearing peace signs, I accept the label with a smile. After all, hippiedom was about getting closer to the earth, being independent, and speaking up for your beliefs and causes. Hippie fashion, like so many others, began as a rebellion against the establishment. It was earthy, ethnic, and artsy—styles I happened to love then, and still do. Yet like any other style, it could become a required dress code if you let it. And our goal is freedom, right?

Living in America, we have an enormous range of choices and prices when it comes to clothing, yet many struggle with the daily decision of what to put on their bodies. For me, our

"Consider the lilies of the field."

Minnesota roller coaster of weather overrules any laws of fashion from Haight-Ashbury or Paris. A two-hour moonlit walk from Camp Menogyn across frozen West Bearskin Lake toward the Canadian border taught me the two keys to never being cold: dress warmly and keep moving. Only when we returned to the camp did we realize it was twenty below zero. Since then, either bundled up or wearing long red underwear beneath my dressy pants and tops, I rarely shiver. In the summer, I happily wear cool dresses. But I'm even happier in my swimsuit in my little gardens and spring-fed lake. On those days when my sweat and the earth mingle in passionate plant procreation, only regular plunges into the rejuvenating water can keep me cool and clean. Braids keep my hair out of the way, while providing, like a pony's tail, a handy way to swish the flies and mosquitoes away from my bare back.

I'm grateful that my hair is still healthy, that long and straight comes back into style every now and then, and that the alchemy of time has slipped silver into my "dishwater blonde" and given me "champagne." (I'm also grateful to my sister for that label—so much tastier than "gray.") I know my simple style doesn't appeal to everyone, but what style does? People are often surprised to hear that I didn't pay big money for that "beautiful natural look." Although I can appreciate gorgeous curls and colors on others, I've never had the patience for that carousel of constant cuts and chemicals. *Hmm*, as many people cover their gray, do the rest of us look older by comparison? Maybe. But I hear the early practice of powdering wigs was an attempt at looking *more* gray—older and therefore wiser. While I think I'll skip the powder, I do hope that my increasing silver will bless me, strand by strand, with a bit of the sage as I age.

Comfort is number one to me. It may have been cold that day, but after snowshoeing, I had to lie down and cool off.

Could it be that our hairs really are like antennae, bringing us wisdom? Research by the military says yes. The extraordinary tracking skills of Indigenous scouts were lessened when given military haircuts. When they were allowed to keep their long hair, their super-sensitive instincts remained. Some say hair gets even more receptive as it gets more silver. The jury is still out on whether hair dye can cause cancers; but to me, that's another reason to skip the time and expense and go natural.

I must admit, for someone who doesn't care much about clothes, I have a lot of them. Some of my favorites are things I've found on the curb or at a secondhand store, but church rummage sales are my mainstay when it comes to shopping. I'm glad to make the contribution to what is usually a good

Mom's church rummage sale — my favorite place to shop.

cause, whether I'm paying the typical two or three dollars for an item or the occasional ten or twenty on something special. I thought a little before I paid twelve dollars for a pair of boots, but they were good quality and I liked them. I liked them even more when I saw an almost-identical pair in a fashion catalogue, for $295. Though I may spend half a day at one of these big friendly sales, I do it only a few times each year, and it's usually a treasure-hunting joy. That was not the case on my recent trip to a "real" store to buy the new underwear I occasionally need. I found myself in a panty jungle, with aisles and aisles of every style and color hanging on little plastic disposable (yuck) hangers. Every style, that is, except what I wanted: good old-fashioned comfy cotton underwear.

Navigating stores and paying full prices drives me crazy, so I rarely do, yet I still function well in the world. Most of my life I've been at ease, whether climbing into a dumpster or meeting Ella Fitzgerald. Friends say it's because I'm comfortable in my own skin. But how do we get that way? I'm sure it's different for everyone, but I'll share a little personal history and philosophy in hopes that it might help you resist that ubiquitous pressure to conform and consume.

Matthew 6:28–29 may be one of the most recognizable Bible verses ever: "And why are you anxious about clothing? Consider the lilies of the field, how they grow; they neither toil nor spin; yet I tell you, even Solomon in all his glory was not arrayed like one of these." (ASV)

Indisputable. Yet I've always envied my cats more than lilies for their clothing. Cats are always impeccably dressed, in exquisitely handsome and infinitely practical lick-and-wear. Sensuous, yet modest, their raiment hides any wrinkles, pimples, or dimples of fat while easily stretching into an extreme ninja move or an elegant ballet. I've always chosen a cat for its personality more than its look, yet each (Spike, my sleek, blue-eyed Siamese; Reno, my rabbit-furred tabby with perfect eyeliner; or Lucky, my black kitten with her little white bikini and two white toes) has been an exclusive design of Mother Nature. Feline fashion rules in my book.

But recognizing my ideal as unattainable, I settle for comfort with as much aesthetic as I can easily muster.

I need to credit my parents. My mother was a skillful and artistic seamstress who loved to sew. What could be more exciting than designing my own prom dresses and making them with Mom? One of my high school jobs was at a fabric store, where I'd find the perfect unique cloth among the remnants. Who needs mice and birds and *bibbidy-bobbidy-boo?* (Remember Cinderella?) The balance came in teaching me that

Spike was always well-dressed and well-behaved. He resisted this nuthatch when I told him "No!"

this was all fun, but not really that important. It was the inside that really counted.

I can remember only one time Dad complimented me on a dress. I guess he just didn't care much about clothes, though he always dressed appropriately. Around the house, he often wore as little as possible. It must be from him that I inherited my warm-blooded nature and determination to escape the swelter that shuts down my body and brain. I do recall his advice to "tuck your tummy in, keep your shoulders back and your chin up."

I guess I resented it then, as teens do parental advice. But many years later I heard a popular musician say, "I'm not a handsome man, but I've learned to carry myself as if I am." Oh, *that's* what Dad meant. I saw it when watching movies. I'd see an actor, thinking he or she had ordinary looks—until a courageous, passionate, or *com*passionate stance transformed the character into a heartthrob. Dad was right, and his advice is becoming even more valuable as I feel the effects of time and gravity.

I rarely shopped, so I was surprised when I was chosen to be on a local department store's Teen Board. There I learned a lot about fashion, makeup, grooming, and modeling, and got to meet girls from many other schools. (I can still recall our "uniform"—the short purple plaid skirt and belted jacket has come back in and out of style since then.)

I was lucky to have that chance to polish my appearance and boost my confidence. But it paled in comparison to the lesson in fashion I got later when I took canoe trips in the Boundary Waters, first as a camper and then as a guide at Camp Menogyn. When you know you'll be carrying everything you bring on your back, along with a hundred-pound canoe, fashion quickly gives way to necessity. Style on the trail might mean choosing between a blue or red bandana—not much more. Since the weather could range from broiling sun to icy sleet, a dry shirt was a real luxury, in *any* color!

It was the sweating as we paddled in sync, the shivering together in the wind and rain, and the laughing and singing around a campfire, that gave us glimpses into one another's and our own hearts, making what was on our bodies irrelevant.

Sure, there was that one guy with a tie, but most of us cared not a whit about fashion at camp.

What a priceless education in style that was. This is not to say that being clean didn't matter. Sharing a canoe and a tent meant smelling fresh *did* impact the quality of our days and nights. But we found that a daily swim in the clear, cold lake and a little deodorant sufficed. Smelly toiletries would only detract from the fragrance of pines and draw swarms of dreaded mosquitoes, if not an occasional bear.

Like my cats, the uncommon beauty of the common loons brought out a bit of envy in me. Their stunningly intricate black-and-white mating plumage, their diamond collars, and their garnet eyes were as mystically beautiful as their thrilling calls. But as our bodies grew stronger and the sun kissed our hair and we recognized the hard-won healthy glow in our smiling cheeks, we all began to feel more and more like Mother Nature's

There was too much true beauty in the Boundary Waters to worry about what our clothes looked like.

beautiful children. That's when I noticed the irony inherent in fancy clothes: they usually inhibit the kind of activities that promote the healthy bodies that emit true beauty. Another truth struck me on a later trip to Florida, where I hardly recognized the loons dressed in their winter grays: even the most fashionable of birds don't *always* dress in formal attire!

Other camps gave me other experiences in fashion, from learning to make authentic Indian bead work on a loom to painting ourselves and a bus and riding it in the local parade, causing some of the townsfolk to wonder if we really were a bunch of hippies. If they'd seen us the day we all turned our bed sheets into togas and weeds into laurel wreath crowns and our little northern camp into ancient Rome, they'd have been totally confused. *Hey*—a meager environment can be the birthplace of creativity!

When I see teens wearing tie-dyed shirts and listening to sixties music, I flash back to these happy times and smile. But my smile fades when I hear that fewer and fewer are embracing the outdoors, while the average American teen spends nearly nine hours a day with electronic media. "Nature deficit disorder" (a term coined by Richard Louv) is a real thing! When I worked at the library, I suggested a young man go outside and enjoy the beautiful day. He'd been on the computer for hours. He replied, "I don't like outside." Oh, dear. Others are afraid, or their parents are. Could their fear stem from having a steady diet of television crime that portrays the woods only as a place to dump bodies? I have rarely been afraid in the woods, even alone at night. But I find it frightening and sad that so many miss out on the outdoors, this powerful portal to physical, mental, and spiritual health. I wish we could take every child into the woods, the lakes, the mountains to experience for themselves the joys and lessons to be learned there.

When I got my first real teaching job, I was awed by the influence I held over my thirty-three first-graders. It was pretty clear their hierarchy was God, Mom and Dad, Teacher. Scary! I did my best to teach them about life as I taught them their ABCs and 1 2 3s. We went outside every chance we got, whether to do our reading in the shade of a tree, or to study the leaves and bark and life cycle of the tree itself. Another part of their education was to see me, this person they looked up to and loved, in many different kinds of clothing. Somehow I knew it was important that they not have just one image connected to that primal figure. So my dress varied from professional suits to peasant dresses to jeans, deliberately teaching them that I was the same person regardless of what I wore; that it was folly to judge people by their clothes. The school principal initially objected, but when I explained my motivation, he couldn't really argue. Later, as a librarian working with many young people, I still made it a point to dress in a range of styles, and to compliment kids on their smiles and behavior more than on their clothing. I sometimes run into my students — adults with their own children now — who remember our first-grade class and say it helped start them on a happy path. Perhaps that focus on character and individuality instead of appearances had something to do with that.

Deciding what to wear and arguing with our teens over clothes are hard enough. The global implications of what we buy can seem too daunting to contemplate. Chinese rivers run blue with dye from jeans while, in India, children's hair turns gray from pesticides on nearby cotton fields. Synthetics made from recycled plastic may have benefits, but they don't biodegrade, and have questionable health effects. We reel if we compare the exploitation of children in dangerous sweatshops with the exorbitant profits and extravagant lifestyles of those at the top. Good grief! Is there any good news? Yes. Global communications and documentaries like *The True Cost* have shone a light on these hidden abuses. Secondhand stores are booming, and greener and fairer alternatives to the fast fashion industry are emerging every day.

What can we do to be a part of the solution? How can we be "cool" on a warming planet? Remember that fashion is fickle by design, depending on the revolving door of style to keep the money flowing. This focus on constant change instead of sustainability uses tremendous resources in production and transportation, while yesterday's fashions end up in landfills. Go

My big brother teased me mercilessly when I wore the tutu Mom made for me at Christmas, but look at how happy I was!

ahead—buy something new when you want it. But not because someone else says your sweater is "so last year."

I believe we can use our amazing range of fabrics and technologies and expand our ingenuity to create a new, more humane, more ecologically and economically rational garment industry. Re-envisioning such a universal and influential entity may seem far-fetched. But we are all part of the culture that supports or rejects it. (Once people realized that no-iron shirts contained dangerous formaldehyde, they demanded better. One manufacturer, Twillory, spent two years developing SafeCotton. I predict others will follow!) Each of us *can* use our consumer power to give ourselves more individuality, more comfort, more self-sufficiency and, yes, more true style. The beauty of our vast market economy is that we can shape our own wardrobes and the corporate climate at the same time; but only with mindfulness and an independent spirit do we find this freedom and power. Replacing in our heads some of the omnipresent corporate images with those of the lily, the cat, and the loon might be a good start.

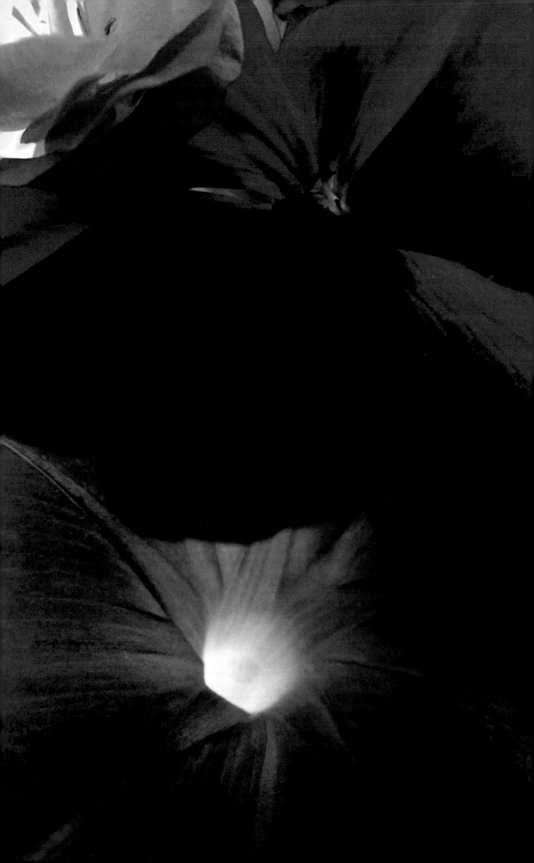

16

Master Class

I was told that red and purple "clashed" and believed it until I saw *West Side Story.* As the young Sharks and Jets clashed at the dance, red and purple swirled into exquisite interplay—stunning, exciting, and forevermore wedded in my mind. Then Maria walked in. She had wanted to be flashy like everyone else, but caring and protective Anita made sure she was the picture of modesty in her simple white dress. Yet Maria stood out above all the rest. What is that elusive quality that makes one fit in and stand out at the same time?

Though parents (and I, too) often cringe at their choices, the business of youth is to find their individual identities and create their own fashions. Choice of clothing is also the privilege of age, as red and purple hats so cheerfully declare. So why shouldn't everyone, from toddlerhood to geezerhood, be allowed personal style?

One of the very few times I made my five-year-old goddaughter cry was when I wouldn't let her wear her good clothes to help out on the sheep farm. Taking my mother to the doctor in her later years meant coming early enough to make sure she

The swirling skirts in West Side Story taught me that red and purple don't clash, and that sometimes white is the most stunning of colors.

had clean clothes on. Adults are often challenged to mentor the young and assist the old while respecting their freedom. Sometimes that means holding up a mirror to their shortsightedness and may save them from embarrassment. Other times it means letting go, or "picking our battles" as they pick out their styles. Either way, encouraging others to let their manner of dress *serve them* is a great gift to give anyone, along with teaching them to respect others' unique tastes. Could that also help narrow the growing chasm between the haves and have-nots? Kids should be able to go out into the world without fear of being shot for their expensive shoes or laughed at for their cheap ones.

The public school I attended as a young child was next to a parochial one, where the students wore uniforms. The prevailing attitude among my schoolmates seemed to be that we were the lucky ones, who could wear what we wanted. Only as I matured did I realize that my luck lay in having parents who, while not having a lot of money, were resourceful enough to provide acceptable and sometimes even "cool" clothing for us. It occurred to me that having required uniforms might free some of my neighbors from the burden of keeping up with the Jones's clothes. But seeing the nuns in their black habits with only hands and faces exposed to the air filled me with dread. I was often miserably hot even in the lightest of clothing. When I heard of early Quakers wearing only wool, I was horrified, until I read that it was originally an act of protest against the cotton industry's use of slave labor. What would I have done?

Decades later, I became close to a young Somali refugee while teaching her to read. Even though some of her long, flowing clothing and hijabs were beautiful, my penchant for breeze on my skin made them seem oppressive to me. (I was glad it was cool and rainy the day we went to the state fair!) But then I began to think of all the women who spend hours every day perfecting their hair, makeup, and dress. I thought of the shape-wear and bras and high-heeled, pointy shoes, and pantyhose, and shaving, and waxing . . . I realized my Muslim friend was free from much of that. So who am I to judge, when physical, stylistic, sexual, and religious freedom depend on the context of our inner and outer lives?

Yet we do judge, consciously or not. I appreciate polite expressions of opinion, so much that I periodically invite friends, ages eight to sixty-something, to help me clean out my closet. "Tell me what you think I should keep or donate, and what you might like to take home!" We have a lot of fun and always conclude that we may as well wear what we like, answering critics with a smile and, "It's okay if you don't like this. I do." I've seen great library books on fashion trends of the past. What a fun way to show kids that what one person calls weird or ugly is often another person's "best dressed" and might even start the next craze.

It's good to have defenses against criticism, but I'm glad to see the rise of "no bullying" campaigns. In my experience, kids who are taught by parents and teachers who don't tolerate meanness feel safer and act kinder. I can't help but wonder how different our wardrobes and lives would be if only we felt accepted, regardless of the color of our skin, our religion, our various abilities and preferences. What if all children were heard, regardless of their language or accent? What if each person's relationship to the divine and to sexuality were recognized as a personal, lifelong work-in-progress?

When I speak to groups of young people, I know some are

wondering, "Does she really get by with just secondhand clothes? Can you really dumpster dive and still have cool friends? You really don't care about brand names?" etc.

To answer them, I share a few stories of people I've known who've become *their own* brands.

Back when my passion for music got ahead of my income, I found I could experience some of the best concerts and theater in town by volunteering to usher. This saved me money and gave me an opportunity to contribute to the arts I loved. Being an usher also got me backstage, where there were always fascinating things to learn and people to meet.

The uniquely mesmerizing sounds George Winston coaxed from grand pianos around the world put him at the center of Windham Hill Records, and sold a lot of albums. When I ran into him backstage at Orchestra Hall in 1983, with his arms full of suitcase, coat, and records, what could I do but thank him for his lovely music and offer to help? He gratefully accepted and there began a friendship that has lasted decades.

If you've seen George in concert, you know he walks on stage stocking-footed and in jeans. That might be common for rock stars, but I suspect it's unusual for a solo pianist at orchestral halls. George and I were born the same year, part of the generation that not only burned bras, but also rejected business suits and ties, girdles and high heels. They were much too restrictive for our free spirits. But his reason seems to be what he said on stage one day: "I welcome your suggestions, unless you want me to wear a tux. I don't have time." When he told me about "breaking up" with his signature plaid flannel shirts and switching to long-sleeved Ts, I started thinking about how much time I could save by limiting my wardrobe to a simple style or two.

George Winston plays at sold-out halls around the world. I love his music and admire his choice to always dress simply. (photo by Sue Lund photography)

But could I do it? I guess I like variety too much to simplify as well as George does, but he and others still inspire me to limit the time I spend worrying about what to wear.

I was just a novice in the world of music and more often sat in with bands as a guest than performed with my own. That meant I had only three minutes in which to make an impression. I'd often seen singers in clothing (or lack thereof) that distracted from the performance. Luckily, I had enough secondhand shopping finesse to look like a million bucks when I needed to — well, maybe a hundred — on my waitress-tip budget. I always tried to dress respectfully, and never found my Secondhand Rose clothes to be a handicap, whether performing, or when approaching my favorite singers, hoping they might consider some of the songs I was writing. Truth be told, most people care more about what you see in *them* than how you look.

Though established artists may not have to bow to fashion,

I respected these musicians and was happy to dress the part of a big-band singer. But I don't recall wearing high heels since.

some are known for their posh appearance. In 1982, when John Lee Hooker graciously agreed to let me "pick his brain" about music, I couldn't help but notice his impeccable attire, complete with fine jewelry and dapper hat. He had come a long way from his sharecropping parents in Mississippi but brought with him the steady rhythm his stepfather taught him on guitar. He put it into hits like "Boogie Chillen" and "Boom Boom" and carried them around the world.

Our plans to talk music changed when we heard that his belongings had been stolen from his motel room. John Lee was so upset that he could hardly speak. I helped him file the police report and took him to the county hospital to order replacements for his missing medications. The next day I picked him up and brought him back to the hospital to get them, then brought him lunch.

It's hard to know if what we are wearing might make us

a little safer or draw misfortune. Mr. Hooker's fine clothes and expensive jewelry fit his status as legendary icon of blues and rock-and-roll. Though his exquisite appearance may have enticed the thief, in no way did it justify the theft, any more than a woman's manner of dress is an excuse to treat her poorly or a child's clothing makes it okay to tease him.

If I had any jewelry on at all, it was likely to be shells, feathers, or stone, as I've never owned a diamond and wouldn't know real gold from a good imitation. But do you think he noticed what I was wearing that day? I doubt it. I didn't get much of a chance to pick his brain about music, but I'll never forget what he said to me: "When you are famous, people are always trying to get what they can from you. You are one of few people who were more concerned about what *I* needed." His words meant a lot to me. That incident was a vivid testimony that all people, despite their fine appearance, success, and status, and sometimes *because* of them, have their times of vulnerability, pain, and need. Perhaps my understanding was why John Lee gave me the privilege of sitting in with his band a few years later.

While freedom for George Winston and me often means casual, comfortable, easy-care clothes, freedom for John Lee and others meant elegance, style, and quality. Each of us has individual and collective histories that give us different needs and goals. Being free means being able to claim our own dreams, our own lifestyles, and even the fashions that feel right to us inside and out.

Encouraging each other, especially our youth, to find and express our own fiery reds and purples or cool whites; our own dusky blacks, elegant blues, or soft pinks; gives us the courage to be ourselves and bring our own special gifts to the dance.

17
The Birthday Gift
of the Tortoise

I grew up believing that my little sister was the cute one so I'd better just try to be smart. It took many years and compliments to boost my confidence in my looks. But my basic belief—that it was the inside that really counted—stayed more or less intact and allowed me to concentrate on more important things.

So I was surprised to find myself looking in the mirror more often as my sixtieth birthday loomed. I'd never been sad or secretive about birthdays. Every year truly is a gift. Why was I feeling a bit apprehensive about this one? I was already enjoying the seniors' discount at the thrift store, and I treasured my many older friends. I'm blessed with health and plan to live a long time, so sixty isn't old in the big picture, right?

I couldn't really blame this gray cloud following me on the man who'd recently entered—and exited—my life. He had told me I was all he ever wanted in a woman, and that I was beautiful. The words from his lips seemed sincere, but I saw no love in his eyes. I became unusually self-critical and sensitive to the endless hype surrounding me. The commercial media offered a thousand and one remedies for lovelessness—for a price, of course.

No, this isn't me, but that's how young I felt in the waves!

The self-examination wasn't all bad. It actually spurred a cleaning of my closet and purging of unflattering clothes—something I'd long been meaning to do. I made a little extra effort to remember to put on mascara before I left for work and do a bit more Pilates. Still, as my sixtieth drew closer, I noticed a new line, a new droop, a little more gray every week.

I decided my January "big" birthday was a good excuse for a Florida vacation. What could be better than long walks on the beach, swimming in the ocean, and writing? Especially when a friend was gracious enough to invite me.

The break from work was as refreshing as the sea breeze and just what I needed. The sweet warm air and sun on my bare arms and legs reminded me that I lived in my body, not just in sweaters. The playful waves attempting to knock me down felt like a glorious massage and made me laugh out loud with the gulls conquering the wind above me. I enjoyed seeing new faces, and exchanging glances, smiles, words. I shared that I was there celebrating my sixtieth, and I appreciated the shocked looks I got from both men and women. Most guessed me to be much younger. What does sixty look like, anyway?

The Japanese garden we visited was the perfect place to reflect on the imperfect and fleeting nature of beauty. It was thrilling to see lions without bars at Lion Country, even if I did get scolded

over a loud speaker for rolling down my window to get a picture! The black tongue of the giraffe I fed at a zoo reminded me of the baby mountain goat who licked my hand in the Rockies so many years earlier.

But I received my very best birthday gift from a giant tortoise. Knowing she might be well over a hundred, I immediately thought, *I want to embrace age. But how?* Who better to ask than this ancient icon of longevity and wisdom?

I sat down on the ground near her. She came closer. I heard a sound like hissing, but saw that her mouth was closed. Could she be greeting me as horses do, by blowing through her nose? I responded in kind. She stretched out her long, strong, gray neck

I felt so trusted by this ancient one as she rested her head on my hand.

and blew again. There were only inches between us. I slowly reached out my hand and rubbed under her chin.

She rested her massive head on my hand. I felt so trusted, so happy to be close to this awesome creature. I whispered to her, *"You're beautiful!"*

I reached under that amazing armor, the stone-gray timeless art that was her shell, and stroked the soft, vulnerable pocket there. I put my hand on her great claws. We gazed at each other for a long time.

I was oblivious to our surroundings until a toddler toddled up to us. I told him yes, "you can pet her," and he patted her head. Another did the same. I thought then that this must be a very calm, friendly tortoise who accepted everyone. But when an adult approached, she pulled her head back into her shell. The woman apologized and left, and the tortoise stretched her head back out to me.

There it was — what I'd always known. It's not about the body, not about the years. These two-year-olds and this sixty-year-old and this ancient one had shared some invisible, invincible link. It's all about the links.

I could have sat there all day, but didn't want to make my friend Elizabeth wait any longer. When I thanked her for her patience, she replied, "Well, it was obvious the two of you were falling in love. I wasn't about to interrupt that! You were clearly bonding."

It was true. I felt connected, not just to that magnificent animal, but to the grace, and patience, and strength, and wisdom, and, yes, the beauty of age.

When I got home to Minnesota and looked in the mirror and saw my neck — what? Is that loose skin? I thought of the tortoise and smiled. When I saw the dry skin on my legs, I put lotion on to preserve a bit of tan, but not before thinking of the same cracked-mud pattern on her well-traveled legs and laughing. The fear of aging that had threatened my psyche was banished by the beauty of that gentle, mighty spirit and the birthday gift she gave me that day.

Only later did I realize that there had been another gift—less pleasant, but a gift nevertheless. To experience that doubt, that lack of acceptance of myself, that sadness at aging, was to be in touch with so many American women in a way that was new for me. Even though I was shy and unsure of myself as a child, it had been a long time since I'd felt that fear—that vulnerability to the media's many messages that we are never quite pretty enough. The warnings to cling to youth and beauty and shiny things—never mind the deeper, freer gifts of nature. The push to spend precious time and money fighting the inevitable instead of honoring it.

Maybe it had been a little too easy for me to scoff at the barrage of magazines where page after page of airbrushed grown-up princesses live happily ever after. Perhaps it took the collision of a little heartbreak and a big birthday to remind me that we are all vulnerable in our own ways, at our own times, to the snake-oil peddlers of the world. And to be thankful for the armor that gives us the strength and peace to laugh at them and turn away. The armor fashioned of links and of love—whether the solid, unconditional love of a parent, the passionate love of a partner who sees the stunning beauty of your soul, or the fleeting but forever love of a tortoise you meet on a bend in life's road.

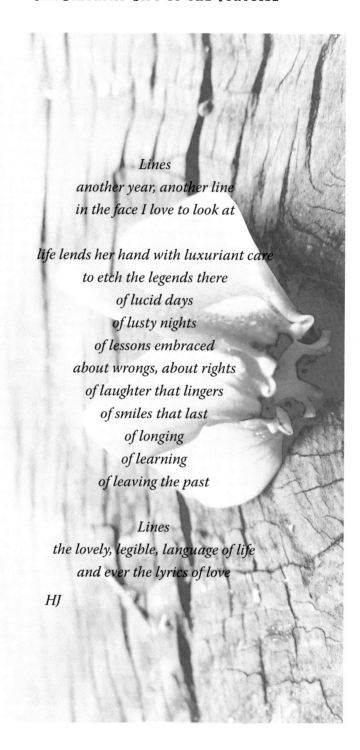

Lines
another year, another line
in the face I love to look at

life lends her hand with luxuriant care
to etch the legends there
of lucid days
of lusty nights
of lessons embraced
about wrongs, about rights
of laughter that lingers
of smiles that last
of longing
of learning
of leaving the past

Lines
the lovely, legible, language of life
and ever the lyrics of love

HJ

18

Dark Chocolate, Maggoty Meat, and

The Marshmallow of Happiness

I imagine you may be wondering if I get my food, like so many other things, from the trash. I don't. (Well, not usually.) Yet I respect freegans–people who eat exclusively out of dumpsters, either out of necessity or to highlight the fact that half the food in this country gets thrown away. Some people even enjoy "Blacktop Cuisine." Though I once pulled a few quills from a dead porcupine, I was not tempted to eat at the Road Kill Cafe.

Do I grow my own? Not much. Living on my wooded glacial moraine is not conducive to growing food. It took me years to discover the one place sunny enough to grow tomatoes–on my dock. But now some critter keeps decimating my crop, regardless of fence and sprays. I admire friends who garden and love it when they generously share their bounty. But for now, I shop at supermarkets, a co-op, a nearby farm, and farmers' markets. The latter are definitely the most fun. Rows of smiling faces behind tables with little trays of brilliantly colored vegetables and fruits—creating, under the blue sky, a patchwork of tantalizing treats for the eye, the tongue, and the body, topped off with dazzling bouquets of flowers.

Will I tell you what to eat? Not a chance. Told that chocolate caused zits and fat, I avoided it for years. Now they tell me that dark chocolate never did cause pimples and actually has heart-healthy antioxidants. Yay! I'm loving this treat . . . Only now I hear it might trigger hot flashes. Darn. Just about every food has it pros and cons, and they seem to change daily. Organics? Vegan? Gluten-free? I don't have a clue what's right for you.

But I do have a key that I found to be very valuable.

I recall, as a teenager, watching a movie in which Anthony Quinn played Inuk, an Inuit man. When a white missionary visited his home in the Arctic, Inuk graciously offered the foreigner their very best food—a bowl of meat crawling with maggots. The missionary was horrified, and Inuk was insulted by his guest's rejection of the delicacy. This brief scene stays in my head today, for it held a powerful epiphany that is confirmed by scientific studies: our tastes are learned.

Mom and Dad always insisted we try one bite of any food, and I recognized this exposure as a good thing. But after that movie, I thought, *Wow! If an Inuit child can embrace a wormy treat, certainly I can learn to prefer green beans over Twinkies.* And I have.

True, my preferences don't extend to chitlins and lutefisk, even though I felt privileged when my African American and Swedish friends shared them with me. I hope never to be offered maggoty meat, but I still find that story so *freeing*. When I can consciously *train* my *tastes*, my choices expand and my need for self-control shrinks. People comment on my self-discipline, but in reality, it's not about denial. I often simply don't want what we're all *told* we want. Rather than accepting the glorification attached to birthday cake and champagne, or the often-maligned reputations of spinach, tofu, or liver, I try to look at everything for what it truly is. Of course I find pleasure in eating (especially popcorn), but I also enjoy good health and the physical ability to do what I please. *That, too, is delicious.* Food that makes me comfortable in my body has become my comfort food.

I remember hating sardines until I'd hiked to the top of a mountain and realized my lunch was still at the bottom. My friend shared his smelly fish with me. Not only was I very grateful for that little tin can of sustenance, but I also suddenly loved sardines! If we never let ourselves or our children get a little hungry, we forfeit the true taste of food and joy of gratitude.

When I heard that cumin was good for me, I tried it. I didn't care for the taste. But I tried it again, and again on something else. Then I threw some in the frying pan with olive oil, garlic, and rosemary to see what they might do for a grilled cheese sandwich. Wow. With a handful of spinach inside, that old childhood lunch has now grown up into a savory delight.

Does healthy eating fit into a lean budget? In my *very* frugal college days, I learned to distinguish between food and entertainment. I might occasionally buy chips, soda, or candy, especially for guests, but I was honest with myself about it being more entertainment than food. When shopping only for myself, it was easy to choose to buy just simple food and save those entertainment dollars for a concert or play. I have more choice now, but still prefer to pay for solid, pleasurable nutrition. I avoid paying to have my food drained of nutrients and cleverly disguised by processing. I prefer "what you see is what you get" to what food writer Michael Pollan calls "edible foodlike substances" gift-wrapped in advertising.

That is not to say I don't believe in the value of presentation. It didn't take many invitations to my neighbor Maxine's lovely

I can't say I'm a great cook, but I do enjoy setting a pretty table, especially when the second-hand choices are plentiful and cheap.

dinners to sell me on cloth napkins and candles, especially since both were plentiful on the curb or at thrift shops. I love enhancing a potluck with a colorful fruit plate garnished with parsley and a single flower from my garden. Somehow it tastes better in one of my (handmade and secondhand) pottery dishes than in plastic. The few dollars is so much better spent on a pot that will last, adding ambiance to a simple dinner enjoyed alone by lamplight or meals shared with friends, than on plastic that will last, but in the landfill.

Balancing budgets with nutritional needs while minimizing waste is a complicated juggling act, especially when our taste buds speak louder than the fine print on the food labels. With endless opinions and studies and ever-changing "facts," all we can do is hear out the experts while listening to our own unique bodies and souls, not judging others, but embracing what rings true for us; being ever grateful for our cornucopia of delights, while advocating for *all* people to have such choices.

Just as there are vast inequities in food availability, there are children with mountains of toys while others have none. But who are the lucky ones? I've told you my favorite childhood toy was Lincoln Logs. I loved creating miniature log cabins reminiscent of the real ones I'd seen at the state fair. Another of my fond memories is of an empty lot. It was not extraordinary, but full of the typical tall grass — aka weeds. My best friend Kim and I would stomp out a square "room" and play house. We twisted the long grass, whether green or dried, into pots and

Did you notice the canister of Lincoln Logs in the picture of me in the tutu? They were my early training for building with real logs.

pans and anything else we needed. If the grass didn't cooperate, we mixed in some mud.

On rainy days, if we weren't splashing in puddles, we'd play in the basement. Ours was unfinished and mostly empty and we loved playing down there on an old metal bed. The mattress, covered in blue-striped ticking, was thin enough to roll up, turning the bed into any vehicle we wanted—a car, boat, or space ship to the moon. We wondered what might happen if we removed that tag "under penalty of law!" When we were tired of traveling, a blanket over the clothesline made a perfect tent. Bedtime meant standing on a chair down there by a heat vent to dry my hair. I was a little spooked, alone in the shadows with only a bare bulb lighting up the ghostly laundry hanging on clothes lines. Good training for camping in the woods.

The basement in our next house was a bit more finished, but not so much that we couldn't share it with Tiki, our husky, or Pinocchio, our duck. Mom and Dad knew what was important. What's a little duck poop, anyway? Though we loved our pets, the responsibility of caring for and cleaning up after them made us think twice before asking for another.

Special days took us to Grandpa's corner grocery, where he'd let us each choose a small treat from the store. There was plenty of candy, but I was more drawn to the glass case filled with stationery items. The paper, pencils, erasers, and mysteries—long wooden pens with strange-looking tips and exotic little bottles of ink—held a creative promise.

Even better was Grandpa's basement, where the fresh smell of cardboard drew us into a small cinder-block room *full* of empty boxes. Maybe it wasn't quite as safe as inflatable rooms full of plastic balls, but it sure was fun, and it was free. I don't know

Somehow I feel we were as excited to go to Grandpa Zahner's corner store as kids are these days to go to the malls full of toys.

if the boxes were destined to be recycled or reused or burned, but they certainly would not have the environmental impact of thousands of plastic balls.

What made all of these "toys" so special? Our imaginations. When we went to the state fair and saw the colorful spin art, I thought of the rotating base of Mom's mixer. She was glad to let us use it, knowing we'd tire of it by the time she was ready to bake a cake. When I outgrew Lincoln Logs, I made miniature houses from boxes, decorating them with found bits of this and that. And of course Mom taught me to make doll clothes from scraps of cloth. When I was old enough to start a neighborhood school in the backyard, the kids and I created a life-sized alligator from paper mache we made from old newspapers. I doubt I'd be upcycling—recognizing the potential in trash and

We had little money to spend at the fair, so we waited until we got home and did spin art on Mom's mixer base.

making so many cool things out of found objects—had I not been challenged with creating my own toys in childhood.

Even when I'm not working with my hands, I'm never bored, for even in the most stark of situations, my mind is busy creating. I am not unique in having developed these talents. Children who are required to *think, wait, and fast* develop patience and skills that serve them and society well. Want proof?

In the late 1960s, Stanford University researchers began an experiment that continued for fourteen years and has been replicated many times. Kids ages three and four were offered a marshmallow. They were told they could eat it if they wanted to, but if they waited fifteen minutes, they would get a second marshmallow, and could eat them both. The experimenters left the room and watched through a one-way window.

My grand-nephew Benjamin, at 4, contemplating the marshmallow.

Some of the kids just ate the marshmallow. Some found ways to resist, like not looking at it, talking to themselves, singing, or another way to distract themselves and make the time pass. Some played with the marshmallow, some licked the table around it, and some put it in their mouths, but didn't swallow. Presenting the gooey blob to the researchers, they proudly said, "See? I didn't eat it!" It must have been a hoot to watch.

The remarkable finding is a strong correlation between the kids' ability to *wait*—to delay gratification—and their future success and happiness. Fourteen years after their marshmallow test, the kids who couldn't wait were more stubborn, envious, and easily frustrated. The kids who waited were more optimistic, dependable, and happier. They even scored an average of 210 points higher on their SATs.

Another study describes similar consequences when children are given too much attention and too little structure. While loving parents rightfully respond to their children's trauma by nurturing, there is a fine line between comforting the child and reinforcing the drama. My parents acknowledged my physical or emotional pain, empathized, and applied a band-aid—or a hug. (Another study showed kissing an owie really does make it heal faster!) Then Mom and Dad moved on, perhaps nudging me toward a healthy distraction, or even sending me to my room to cry—allowing me to get it out *and* get over it. Children in the first year or two of life need a lot of attention to develop lasting emotional security. But we need to follow that up by teaching them to comfort themselves, deal with disappointment, and let it go. This is a gift that will help them grow into happy, resilient adults.

So what is the marshmallow of happiness? The second marshmallow. The one you have to wait for, to work for, to achieve. When Siddhartha, on his path to enlightenment, listed "I can think, I can wait, I can fast," as his valuable skills, he was predicting the results of the marshmallow experiment! While we don't need our children to suffer the skin-and-bones asceticism he did, we'd do well to remember that it was *going without,* not riches, that freed the prince from want and gave him his contented and compassionate smile.

You may be familiar with the traditional lullaby, "Hush, Little Baby." The lyric promises gift after gift, from a mockingbird to a diamond ring and many more.

That song was a mother's expression of deep love for her child. The gifts were metaphorical, expressing the endlessness of her love. Like many others have done before me, I rewrote the lyrics and music:

Hush, little baby, don't say a word,
Listen to the song of the mockingbird
And if that mockingbird won't sing
We'll make her happy with a song we bring
Hush, little baby in my arms
You have the wealth of an angel's charms
And as you grow in love and truth
Heaven will shower blessings over you
You won't need a looking glass
If you treat the world with care
Look in the eyes of the ones you love
Your beauty is reflected there
Hush little baby don't you cry
You'll see the whole world bye and bye
And if that world seems poor and cold
You'll warm it up with a heart of gold

HJ

I'm grateful that my parents were able to provide me with the necessities as well as some things just for fun. But it means even more to me that, as young parents with no instruction manual or studies to guide them, they knew enough to give me the greater gifts of patience, self-sufficiency, creativity, and gratitude—the marshmallows of happiness.

19
Why Did the Computer Cross the Road?

Because it Was Programmed by the Chicken

I found that joke on the internet, credited to nine-year-old Shelley in New South Wales. Pretty profound for a nine-year-old, and for a joke, and for a chicken! Profound because it raises the question, who programmed you and me? Why are we compelled to consume as much as we do? How are we programming our children? What does it mean for their future and ours?

We probably have some inborn instinct to acquire things. I hear that monkeys are often caught by simply putting an apple or banana in a box with a small hole. The monkey will put its hand in and grasp the treat, and being unable to withdraw its full hand, will be captured rather than relinquish the treasure. I feel that way on some days spent cleaning the garage or basement—sacrificing my freedom because I can't let go of all that stuff. You've probably heard a rich man's odds of heaven (or happiness?) compared to a camel's chances of passing through the eye of a needle—an actual gate into Jerusalem, through which a camel couldn't pass if its pack was too wide—a nice analogy for all of us burdened with too much stuff.

I don't blame all our acquisitiveness on advertising, but I do think it was auspicious that my favorite places drew me out

"As if you could kill time without injuring eternity."

of the house and away from the media. There are holes in my awareness of pop culture; I missed songs, news events, gossip, and trends during whole summers in the woods or at the beach. I was happy to hear the reassuring phrase, "Anything of true artistic value will come around again," and I look forward to recapturing those few summer losses in my autumn years. I do enjoy a bit more TV in the winter, but when people ask where I find the time to do my endless projects, the fact that "I ain't hip" to the newest shows and don't have cable is a clue. I'm so glad I happen to prefer public radio and television. That means I get to skip the ads—and not look at the marshmallow. The average urban American sees or hears about 5,000 commercial messages a day. Five thousand a day, 365 days a year. That's a lot of marshmallows to resist.

But it's not just advertising that programs us to spend. Almost all media presents a constant parade of enticing images: dramatic moments, handsome faces, housing makeovers. I can get sucked in as quickly as anyone else, so I try to periodically reclaim my attention and ask myself, "Do I really need to know this? Am I really enjoying this or is it making me tense? Will I feel enriched after watching this, or resent the time wasted?" Even silly entertainment can be a needed escape, but there is always a trade-off. I can count on a lavender sunset to make me happy, but TV? Not so much. "As if you could kill time without injuring eternity," Thoreau said in Walden in 1854. Our ubiquitous media just makes the murder easier.

Has "SAVE" come to mean "spend," but just a little less than you *might* have spent? Did you have a piggy bank when you were little? Was it easy to put money in and hard to get it out? Mine was a blue and gold ceramic pig. I remember spending afternoons with a knife trying to coax the coins out of the slot, just to count them, of course. I'd never have considered breaking that gift from Grandma. I still have it.

Later my parents instituted the bank box. We divided a cardboard cheese box into three sections. Half of every dollar I got went into the first part, for college, and was periodically deposited into a real bank. A quarter went into the five-dollar bank, to be spent only when the contents totaled that magic number. The remaining quarter was mine to spend as I pleased. When "playing school" evolved into my own backyard daycare, I charged a quarter a day for each of the dozen or more kids and got lots of practice moving money around.

That bank box was one of the best gifts my parents ever gave me. Even though I couldn't spend the money in the "real" bank,

The piggy bank Gramma Bea gave me is prettier, but the bank box Mom and Dad required of us kids taught me more.

I could see it growing and earning interest. Wow—free money! By the time I started college, I had $2,000 in that fund. That was a lot of quarters back then, and I might not have gone to college without it. (Then there were the premiums for opening or adding to your account. I still have the set of stemware that I built, with the help of family and friends, one account and four glasses at a time.) Neither interest rates nor free gifts are as valuable as they were back then, but the lessons certainly are.

The five-dollar bank taught me to *wait* and to *think* about every purchase. Often by the time I had saved the required amount, I decided I didn't really want that umbrella, or that I wanted a new bedspread more. I did spend some of that fourth quarter on penny candy when I rode my bike to the neighborhood store, but it didn't take long to realize I could put it in the five-dollar bank instead and get that "big" money out much sooner. (Besides, sucking those little candy dots off the paper and that colored sugar out of the straws got old, remember?)

To this day when I consider buying something expensive, or even a small purchase that most people wouldn't hesitate to make, my inner voice says "Yes, I can buy this, or I can put this quarter in the other box and get something bigger and better—like security, time, freedom!"

As a person with virtually everything I really want and *no debt*, I must say this little voice has served me well. I do spend money, and time, and energy, but I do it mindfully. I'm sure people have sometimes thought I'm too cheap to buy what everyone else is buying, but it's usually because I don't want it, at least not enough to make the inevitable trade-off. And—this is a big and—I long ago stopped feeling I should buy something just because everyone else is doing it. I'm not embarrassed to order soup in a restaurant if that's all I want, even if everyone else is having steak and drinks.

So "shop 'til you drop" never appealed to me. I've largely avoided shopping malls, with the regrets and returns that often follow. But in all honesty, I remember many a day I'd stop at the thrift store after visiting Mom in the nursing home. I knew she was unhappy and the unanswerable questions of what to do weighed heavily on my heart and mind. I began to understand why so many people use shopping as a stress-reliever. Just browsing through the aisles, seeing the plethora of goods, and thinking about whether to buy some little thing or not was so much easier than facing the overwhelming decisions about

Mom's care. The last time I stopped just to wander through the used but interesting treasures was after spending a day at the hospital with a dying friend. I didn't buy a thing, but felt myself decompressing as I wandered the aisles among strangers, knowing the next day I'd be tasked with calling friends with the sad news. Luckily, that therapy cost me little. But since Mom passed and it fell to me to empty her house, then seeing my friend's house full from years of collecting, and thinking of my own and not wanting to burden others when it's my time to go, shopping of any kind has even less appeal. Now I only stop in if there's something I need, and only on senior discount days!

While I don't spend much at stores, I've invested a lot of money and even more time on my own creative pursuits. I wrote dozens of songs and recorded many with the help of fine musicians. It felt good to pay them when I could; sometimes they generously donated their time. I studied the business, copyrighted everything, and sent out tape after tape, with carefully written letters. I was thrilled when one of my songs was recorded by a national group, but painfully disappointed when I never got a cent or even proper credit. Still, the joy and experience of working with gifted, bighearted, local musicians is a treasure, something I'll never regret. Some of those songs ended up in "Looking-Glass Love Songs," a play I wrote and produced with lots of help from family and friends. Grants, along with the gracious support of Mixed Blood and At the Foot of the Mountain theaters (and modest ticket sales) kept me out of the hole. I learned so much and was able to pay the talented director, technician, actress, and musicians with whom I was privileged to share the stage.

I can't begin to describe how much I and many others put

Can you tell how much fun we had creating The Quitnots? Jerry Thomas generously provided us with our own John Wayne and his favorite pig when we shot a scene at his Diamond T Ranch.

into *The Quitnots*, my dream of a children's television series. We got as far as the preview before a sliding economy and the pressure of my father's illness derailed it. But what an experience. How could I regret those investments, or any of my other creative pursuits? Though my collection of rejection letters *could* be seen as a painful failure, they were often encouraging and never stung as much as when I invested my hard-earned money and the stock market crashed. My projects, and the many generous artists who believed in them, have all developed my skills, knowledge, and confidence. These, along with lasting friendships, are dividends I can bank on in lean or better times.

You may ask, what about gifts? Don't you have to go to the mall to buy gifts?

Do you remember your favorite childhood gifts? My first ones were dolls and the cute clothes Mom made for them. While other kids were torn between their teddy bears and Barbie Dolls, my bed was adorned with a plush octopus. At Christmas, I *loved* my new pajamas. I couldn't wait to curl up under the tree in them, the flannel as soft as the glow of the multicolored lights, its fresh scent wafting with that of balsam fir.

My favorite clothes, along with most of my gifts, were chosen or made by Mom. But later, when I was living in my log cabin and loving my stone fireplace, Dad bought me a great little bow saw. He sharpened an old ax blade, painted it red, and put a new wooden handle on it. Then he made a simple little sawhorse. I still use these to cut and split my firewood, and I get a warm feeling every time I do. It's not just the body heat of hard work, but the heartwarming knowledge that Dad knew me better than I thought he did and admired my strength and independence. The trick of great gifting is to listen to the person you're buying *for* more than the people you're buying *from*.

Americans tend to have generous spirits, and I don't want to criticize generosity. But I *will* expose a sad truth — I've found *sooo* many things at rummage sales, secondhand stores, and in the trash that I just know must have been gifts. It seems to me that gift-giving has become the vine, planted with good intentions, that overgrows the house and keeps out the light. It helps to remember that generosity and frugality are not mutually exclusive. Nor are affluence and prudence. Sometimes the best gift is no gift, the best prize is no prize.

Do I ever give secondhand gifts or, heaven forbid, gifts from the Curbside Boutique? Yup, occasionally, and especially when I find things in the original box or with the tag still on.

This darling coat was in the trash, but still had the tag attached. I gave it to a friend for her new granddaughter.

If they are appropriate, and *if* I believe the recipient will like it and would not be shocked to know its source. (Most of my friends wouldn't.)

I've been surprised more than once when someone has said, "You give the best gifts!" Well, sometimes they *are* unique. I don't always reveal my sources, but I know doing so might be an additional gift—permission for them to do the same. Many of my friends know that I might *prefer* something used to something that uses more of the earth's resources.

My family always recognized gifts from Aunty Holly by their wallpaper wrapping; more unique and sturdier than thin wrapping paper, and far less expensive when picked up as leftover rolls. The vinyl pieces can live on as drawer or shelf lining. I've taped or pasted gorgeous calendar art to paper bags with

This wallpaper may be out of style for walls, but still makes sturdy, unique wrapping for gifts. Tape calendar pages to bags to make your own unique gift bags. Maps make perfect wrapping for those graduates and retirees off to see the world.

handles for unique gift bags. I've had fun peeling the paper from oatmeal boxes (the cheaper ones work better) and decorating the earthy brown cardboard underneath. A twine or ribbon handle makes it a strong, handsome gift bucket. But I think my favorite is using old maps for wrapping, especially for avid travelers or teens heading off to college with their dreams.

I see less of any kind of wrapping these days, more often receiving and giving gifts that don't require any. The first such gift I got was from Katie and Brad — an acre of cloud forest in South America. Wow! Nothing to take up space in my little home, just the mental image of that misty land saved from deforestation. I was thrilled. Next came my brother's card saying a dozen fluffy yellow chicks had been given to a needy village in my name. Nice! He started a tradition I was glad to continue—llamas, bunnies, bees. Then there was a tree planted in Israel from my friends the Lunds. There are dozens of ways to honor a friend or loved one while giving to those neighbors, local or global, who are truly in need. Ways that bring lasting benefits and awareness instead of momentary laughter and a lifetime in the landfill. For those who want to make a donation in someone's name but still give something tangible, there are many such options. The stuffed toy that a child cuddles can remind her that an endangered animal is being helped. I love buying the handmade pottery of the Empty Bowl projects and filling them with treats. My family gets the bowls, while the profit goes to fight hunger.

Then there are the gifts that don't require money. My family has long given coupons for things like housecleaning and back rubs. One year, I promised to make Dad's bag lunches whenever I was at their house on a weeknight. That pleased him and Mom. My niece Kym gave us a handmade cookbook full of her scrumptious recipes. *Yum.* As we age, it becomes ever more clear that time and an open heart are our most precious gifts. Even a dog knows that.

As I was typing this chapter, my part-time canine, Java, very deliberately dropped her ball on my keyboard, writing k9—honest! Clearly she was saying, "How about paying some attention to the dog!" She was right on two accounts. It was time for a break, and the best gift anyone can give another being—human or not—is attention.

I know it can be really hard to resist giving gifts, especially to kids. Consider giving experiences instead of things—gifts that will make them more *in*quisitive, rather than *ac*quisitive.

A trip to a farm can be a fabulous gift for young or old.

Outings to museums or farms or camping trips don't have to cost a lot, but may give them memories that last a lifetime.

While I was a student at the U, I was a "big sister" to young David through a program at the Y. I didn't have a lot. I shared an old apartment on Seven Corners with three other girls. But I felt rich compared with David who shared a tiny house, also on the Mississippi's West Bank, with his family. I knew it was important to build our relationship on experiences he could continue on his own. I'll never forget the time we took the bus downtown to the library and planetarium, famous for the mummy that was there. What young boy wouldn't want to see a mummy?

But even more exciting was what happened as we walked around town. Passing a store, we saw a crew hauling dozens and dozens of giant mums, with two-foot stems and heads as big as David's, out into a truck. After only a moment's hesitation,

I asked them what was happening. They were removing the decorations after a special event and were happy to give us all we could carry. Imagine the joy David felt at giving an armful of spectacular, wildly fragrant blooms to his mother. I felt the same sharing mine with my mom and hoped the day's good fortune was an omen for David's future. I still have trouble passing up perky flowers in the trash, and I'm never embarrassed to pick them out from the wilted ones. Their lives are so short as it is, and each seems a small miracle of beauty that I am privileged to enjoy, if only for a day or two.

A computer cannot choose the chicken that programs it, but we can, if we keep our eyes and minds open. While we may have been programmed to glorify "progress," we can ask ourselves whether the latest novelty actually *progresses* toward real health, happiness, and sustainability. While we are programmed to give

Even in her wheelchair, Mom loved our trips to the zoo.

and accept gifts graciously, we can strive to make those gifts more meaningful and less costly to our pockets and to the earth. We can opt to accept, and even prefer, "used and imperfect" instead of "new and improved."

(Okay—I admit some friends once sat on a wooden bench on my deck and it slowly collapsed. We laughed, but I noted the difference between rustic and dangerous and . . . my phone just rang—I was just about to write that I needed to upgrade my patio furniture, but it was my friend Deb offering me her unneeded, but very sturdy, attractive patio table and chairs in exchange for doggy-sitting Java. *Hmm*—coincidence or manifestation? Who knows?)

As I was saying, we can replace the pressure to compete with the desire to share. We can choose to value a house as a home, a place to live and grow in a community, rather than primarily as an investment or as a cash machine. We can decide that saying "no thank you" to advertising that insults our intelligence is not about depriving ourselves; it's *freeing* ourselves. We can say no to manufacturing that disrespects the earth, knowing it's not about slowing the economy, but encouraging alternatives and saving the planet. If enough of us ignore advertising we don't like, it will go away. If we buy only what we really want and need, the false and flimsy parts of the economic flock will be culled, while those of true value will thrive. In good or bad times, both economic and ecological, we have plenty of reasons to consciously say "*Whoa!*" to the cult of accumulation and "*Aah, yes!*" to simplicity and sustainability. We have an opportunity to become more truly ourselves, rather than cogs in the wheels of consumption and waste. We can rest gratefully in the bosom of sufficiency.

20
Tips for Shopping at the Curbside Boutique

Wait! Before you are tempted to skip this chapter, I'll start with tips on what to do with your excess "stuff."

I wrote the original version of "Oh, the Things You'll Find at the Curbside Boutique" on Mayday 2008 and was happy when the Minneapolis *StarTribune* opinion page published it. My hope was that readers would think about donating their unwanted goods rather than putting them on the curb, destined for landfills.

Since then, I've been thrilled to see the media full of variations on that theme—the wisdom of reuse—popularized by both economic volatility and by concern for the environment. Whatever their motivation, countless journalists, economists, and people "on the street" now encourage Americans to embrace frugality—whether by cleverly recreating their wardrobes, shopping at secondhand stores, or simply doing without. A *Newsweek* reporter spent a month living as a "freegan" while upscale designers rave about reclaiming architectural treasures. This is a good thing. Ideally, the media's reuse messages will popularize

This arbor looked like junk on the curb, but here it is, welcoming folks to my shore just a few weeks later!

that Depression-era conservation mentality and someday I'll find nothing of value on the curb, but we have a long way to go.

Foreclosures, moving, downsizing, divorce, death, or just too much stuff—there are many reasons to lighten our loads. You may feel overwhelmed and tempted to throw everything out on the curb, but take a second look before you toss. Once while I considered a curbside lamp, a woman called out from the house, "You don't want that lamp!" But it was only to let me know it didn't work. There was a brand-new lampshade on it, still wrapped in cellophane. I asked if the bulb worked, and she said, "I don't know." I took the bulb (it did work) and the lampshade and wondered why the woman saw the whole kit and caboodle as a loss.

I know that many people put items out assuming anything of value will be rescued. I'd like to believe that, but my experience proves otherwise. Many mornings I've been out just ahead of the garbage trucks and seen perfectly good furniture get crushed. So please, think ahead and donate. Thrift stores are so popular these days that they are begging for your castoffs. Check your community's Green Guide or go online for links to organizations that will make sure your discards benefit others. Many will even pick up your donations and leave you a receipt for tax deductions. What a deal!

Some communities ask you not to put your appliances out until morning to avoid having scavengers cut the cords for the copper. Good idea. (Pickers—don't cut cords. Give the item a chance to be used or repaired.) If you are putting out any appliances, attaching a note about whether it works is extremely helpful and appreciated. (Big thanks to the person who put that "WORKS GREAT!" note—on my "new" microwave!) If you have smaller items, consider using open boxes, or clear plastic bags instead of black ones. That way, rescuers can see what's there and are less likely to tear open the trash bags and scatter the contents. If your community doesn't have curbside pickup days, putting usable items out on the curb with a free sign often works well to find them a new home.

Now what about cruising for junk? Still can't picture doing that? I understand the hesitation. While checking dumpsters I used to mentally rehearse the line, "Oh, I'm just looking for boxes because I'm getting ready to move." But I never had to use it. No one ever asked what I was doing, and I came to realize folks were more worried about people putting things *into* their dumpsters than taking things out. Many European countries have a tradition of residents putting things out on the curb every Thursday with the expectation that their neighbors will rescue what they can use before the trash hauler comes. So you could think of yourself as continental. Or maybe you're conducting research or just out for a walk. If you need an excuse, go for it. Or just trust me and try it. I've found many people to be happy that I'm rescuing their castoffs.

A homeowner saw me looking at a chair on his curb and called out, "Wait! I'll get you the seat for that," adding, "Can you use a mailbox? I have a brand new one in the garage." It was lovely, covered in cedar slats, and graced my driveway until I replaced it with a bigger, sturdier one, also found on the curb.

I can still see the face of a classy lady, in expensive clothes and meticulous makeup, walking her little white poodle down her suburban street amid the "Curbside Boutique"—one very different from her usual boutique, I suspect.

I smiled and said, "Hi," but got only a nose in the air in

response. Oh, well. I was years past letting anyone make me feel embarrassed to be junking. But a few minutes later she was walking back, lovely lampshade in hand! Her smile and voice bubbled with excitement as she said to me, "Look what I found!" It made her day, and she made mine. One good find can make you comfortable searching or might even get you hooked.

Just as you do on a shopping trip to the mall, make a list of what you'd like to find. Look around your house and yard with a mind to what's missing, what you'd be tempted to buy if you were at the store. Measure the available space for large items; bring a paint sample if you want it to match a wall or carpet. Sound silly? Well, you've read about my uncanny way of finding what I need and more. Whether or not you subscribe to the "law of attraction," you are more likely to get what you want in life if you know what it is and are willing to search for it. Hold the image in your head and you're more likely to recognize it when you see it, even in a sea of trash.

While thinking of what you want, please think of others, too. Every year there are a few who tear through boxes and bags, scattering the contents on lawns and streets. Maybe the concepts of neatness and trash seem unrelated, but they're not. Broken glass, sharp metal, and moldy or contaminated garbage can become a hazard for children, other rescuers, and the garbage haulers. There IS such a thing as *real* trash, and it needs to be contained.

If you can't quite appreciate the aesthetic of nicely organized junk as you're cruising by, think of the people in the houses, living with the mess for several days. The haulers hired to pick up the stuff have a hard enough job without having to gather up whatever thoughtless people have scattered. It doesn't take much wind to blow loose paper, plastic, and mysterious matter into backyards, woods, storm sewers, and streams. Let's not give the authorities any reason to ban the practice of salvage—it's a good thing for all if done respectfully and safely.

What to wear while cruising? Work clothes. Perfect is an outfit that doesn't make you feel like a bum yet won't suffer from a little dirt or a possible rip or two. Wear gloves and bring along a few tools: a claw hammer, flat and Phillips screwdrivers, an adjustable wrench, even a saw. You may find a great thing attached to a not-so-great thing by a few screws or a bolt. A measuring tape is helpful for large items as well as those discarded jeans—since there won't be a dressing room out there.

These were all clean and folded in a bag on the curb, headed for the landfill. I brought them to a homeless shelter.

If you can, pick up all the good clothing and pass it on to a homeless shelter. You'll feel even better than when you find something cool for yourself.

A trailer or truck is priceless for cruising. My frugal and wealthy neighbor, Donna, offered to take me in her brand-new truck. We had a ball. I still have the marble table we found—thank goodness we had four hands and a four-by-four! Letting a shyer friend drive while I happily trot along the curb checking out the piles is efficient and makes loading treasures much easier. But if you are alone, don't be timid about asking passersby to help you lift. It may be just the introduction they need to cruising.

If you don't have a truck, a tarp on your backseat and some big plastic bags can let you rescue dirty landscaping materials without trashing your car. I've found thirty-dollar ceramic pots, usually with dirt in them, and sometimes perennials waiting to be awakened with a little TLC. Rope, bungee cords, a blanket, or that rug you just found can turn your car top into extra cargo space for those awkward large finds. Just make sure they're not too heavy for you or your vehicle to handle safely, and secure them well . . . And remember it's up there before driving into your garage. (I'm embarrassed to admit it, but I once forgot and busted a nice bamboo loveseat!)

Besides gloves, bring water and hand cleaner, just in case. An old towel and a rag or two are sure to be useful. Since each find tempts you to go "one more block," you'll probably be out longer than you expected, so a few snacks and a water bottle may pick you up while adding a picnic flair to your outing. Create a fitting soundtrack for your adventure with your favorite music, but keep the volume unobtrusive. Oh, and don't forget to bring

A blanket and rope made it easy to bring this arbor home.

Snacks and music make cruising for junk even more fun.

Did I need this worn-out birdcage? Definitely. I discovered it on the curb three days after Mom died. It was the perfect symbol of her escape.

the new, true mind-set: you are not cheap — you are resourceful. You are saving money while saving the earth. You are a salvager, like those brave divers rescuing treasures from sunken ships.

If you're worried about ending up in a fight over some treasure, don't be. I've never seen it happen. More likely is, "Here — you can have it." "No, you take it!" Maybe there's something about all that free stuff that makes competing for it seem laughable. Or maybe junkers are just good, nice, down-to-earth folks.

For me, the most challenging part of cruising for junk is making decisions. Though I always find perfectly good items, many have a flaw, a missing piece, the wrong color. What imperfection can I live with? Is it wabi sabi or just trashy trashy? Do I really have time to renovate it? Can I repurpose it — create something entirely new and wonderful from it? Can my friend use this, or can the church sell it at their rummage sale? Will the next scavenger need or love it more? If I bring it home, it may just become a burden. Perhaps it really is time to lay it to rest in the Shady Hills landfill. Letting things go is a vital part of the art of salvage.

The most important tools of all? A smile and a sense of humor. Take these along and I can almost guarantee you'll have some fun. Keep your eyes and imagination open and you'll see more interesting and even intimate stories than on your favorite soap opera. While you're out there accepting this manna from heaven, accept also that the angels who put it there have any number of reasons for letting their lives spill out onto the curb. Rarely is anyone looking out the window of the house, but I always look up with a smile and a "Thank you" before I leave with their gifts.

21

Price Tags and Tea Bags

Though one man's trash is another man's treasure, in my case, you could say one woman's excess is another woman's emporium, since I choose to acquire almost everything I need or want from what others *don't* need or want. But the question of how we value things deserves a deeper look. Especially as people spend less and less time outdoors and more and more in malls or shopping on the internet, what kinds of price tags do we attach to the world around us?

My good friend Sue reminded me that sentiment often determines the value of an item. When she was missing her daughter who was across the country at college, she'd put on her blue and pink sweatshirt—her half of the matching pair they bought together in Maine. She instantly felt Sarah's arms around her. My niece Kym had so many T-shirts with logos of athletic events that Mom made them into a quilt. Though she'd outgrown the shirts, she will never outgrow the memories.

My grandmother's old earrings hold warm thoughts of our times together, and mysteries of her single days when music was her joy. She once danced with Nat King Cole, not even realizing who he was until after the dance! Was she wearing

He came from Mother Nature and will return to her.

Gram's earrings and Dad's wedding band—not expensive, but precious to me.

these? They're not real diamonds and emeralds, but are they infused with the magic of a real star?

Those earrings and their sentiment don't take up much space in my jewelry box. But memories can add weight to our "stuff" and bind it to us. It seems I always have "clean out closet," or garage, or basement, on my to-do list. Remembering how Mom made that pillow for me or that an old boyfriend gave me that shirt makes it harder to let go of them. I'm learning to trust my journals and photos to hold my memories and rescue me from at least some of my possessions.

On the other hand, feelings may blind us to the simple nature and usefulness of an object. One spring day in 2011, I found a sealed package of beautiful napkins at the Curbside Boutique. The silky paper was embossed with a flourish of silver roses celebrating the fiftieth anniversary of Eva and Rudy. The party was in 1987. Where had these lovely napkins been for twenty-four years? And what emotional connections relegated them to the curb rather than the table? I scooped them up and used them for dessert napkins at my next dinner party, sharing the story as I passed them out to my guests sitting by the fire. Not one of my friends blinked an eye at their origin. Dear-hearted Marcela stood and raised her glass—"to Eva and Rudy!" We all stood and joined in the happy toast, honoring them with our warm laughter.

When Curt and Julie came and saw the pieces I'd salvaged from their old house and the cabin I rented from them, we shared a flood of memories and mutual appreciation. The old boards, windows, shutters, and shelves may have been "junk" for the brief time the house and cabin sat empty awaiting the bulldozer, but no longer. If you can really *use* the items as well as embrace the sentiment, there is a sweet salvation in salvaging well-made things. One that should be evangelized.

When friends complimented me on a dress, I'd often tell them that I paid only a few dollars for it at a rummage sale. Mom would remind me later, "You don't have to tell people that."

But I couldn't resist celebrating a great find. I even told people, when they loved that fuchsia dress with a few blue flowers gracing the skirt and shoulder, that I painted them there—to cover a stain. While the stain threatened to diminish the value, the hand-painted flowers enhanced it. In time, Mom proudly said, "My daughter's a junker!" She loved to cruise the Curbside Boutique with me.

I thank her for raising me on garage sales, which taught me to recognize quality. Still, sometimes I opt for quirky, useful, or fun, regardless of quality. When there are mountains of things to choose from for dimes and quarters, you learn to discern and decide *for yourself* what has value *for you*, regardless of price and without an ad telling you what's "cool." What a liberating and powerful gift that is! Even more precious was my parents' admonition to look for what's of value *inside people*, ignoring the labels others might imagine on their clothing, color, status, or jobs. Just as a bit of soap or new surroundings can make a found object into a treasure, an open heart and non-judging eyes can turn an acquaintance into a friend.

When I turned sixty, my mother gave me a beautiful necklace, handmade by a friend of a friend. The unique triangular stone held the deep blues, greens, and browns of the earth and was artfully fringed with silver and glass beads. By gold and diamond standards, it wasn't expensive, but was certainly the most valuable piece of jewelry I had owned, and I loved it. Loved it and

My favorite necklace became even more special after surviving months under ice.

lost it. After searching everywhere, I thought it must lie some-where under the heavy blanket of snow and prayed it would emerge with the spring flowers. Sure enough, the first torrential rain freed it from its glacial bed, where I'd been driving over it for half the winter! The ice had hidden and protected it, and I cried with joy at the return of this special gift. I also felt lucky that I had rarely suffered that kind of disappointment and guilt at losing something of value. I'd lost or broken or ruined things, of course. But since most of what I owned cost little or nothing, it wasn't a big deal. I'd certainly endured loss, but rarely did loss of *material* things matter much to me. That's another reason cheap is good.

One winter I saw a snowman that was ten feet tall and just as wide. I'm talking about a genuine *snow*man, made of real, natural snow. There was no price tag, but certainly it represented quite an investment. It tickled me to think of how much fun and camaraderie must have gone into building it. How much fresh winter air the snowball-rollers breathed while working every muscle in their bodies. How well they must have slept with that pleasant exhaustion. How good they must have felt sharing their creativity with the neighborhood and those of us who went out of our way to see it. How well the melting of their mammoth sculpture measured the coming of spring, white melting into green, reviving the long-dormant grass.

All around, there were beige plastic snowmen needing storage in the attic or being forgotten until they looked sad and silly on snowless lawns. But not this one. Its end was graceful and useful.

I realize that not everyone is blessed with enough real snow for a snowman or trees that turn to ice-crystal chandeliers under a streetlamp. But it's worth remembering that there are bright, shiny alternatives to plastic decorations that fill stores every year and end up, sooner or later, in the trash. Not that I'm immune to the temptations of "cool" things. Being an infrequent shopper does limit my exposure to enticements (*don't look at the marshmallow*), but I can get as excited as the next person when running across a clever or handy or lovely new thingy.

That was the case when my neighbor Mary showed up with a little plastic battery-run fan on a cord around her neck. My hot flashes spoke up and said, "I need one of those!"

Being a generous soul, she took it off and slipped it over my head, insisting I keep it. I resisted, but not enough to convince her, and finally accepted it, with gratitude. When I wore it to work the next day, my boss pointed out that it made noise. She was right. Catching my image in the mirror, I realized the red and white plastic wasn't exactly a fitting fashion statement for my earthy nature. And it required a battery. Of course you had to hold it up to get the little breeze to go where you needed it. I had *wanted* this. What was I thinking?

I got home and saw, on my shelf, the delicate, old-fashioned blue fan a friend had brought me from China. Had it been made in a factory next to the one making the red plastic fan? Or perhaps it was made in a home, a traditional skill passed on from earlier generations. Were its lacy cuts made by lasers or by hand? I don't know, but surely the graceful branch of pink cherry blossoms had been hand-painted. It was made of bamboo and silk and a tiny metal pin upon which its webbed fingers turned — all wabi sabi materials that may fray with use, but would ultimately return to the earth from whence they came.

There is a reason these fans have been used for centuries; a reason women flirt behind these enchanting little veils, which

A simple silk fan is lovely, useful, and can return to the earth.

can bring out the mystery in one's eyes or expose a smile with
the flick of a wrist. They work! With just the slightest effort

and a comfortable rhythm, beauty is surpassed by function—
a cooling, silent breeze. A bit like the breeze on the porches
where neighbors sat on swings and greeted friends out for
their evening walks, before air-conditioning closed our doors
and treadmills confined our walks to six square feet of rubber.

Do the price tags on snowmen and fans tell us anything about
their true values? What are the true costs and benefits to the
well-being of everyone and everything in the immense loop of
manufacturing, delivering, consuming, and disposing?

I'm not the only one pausing to question the value of our multitude of possessions. In Michael Zadoorian's novel *Second
Hand,* the character J (his girlfriend calls him J for junk) owns
a secondhand shop and has a penchant for the junk he gathers
to resell. Even after he inherits enough money to retire, he continues his rounds of estate sales, noting the difference between
wanting to go junking and needing to. His observations are
worth noting: "At some point in time, people sincerely wanted
to own all the stuff I find so amusing. They coveted and saved
for that pink granite bowling ball . . . sacrificed other things to
get these . . . now all junk." (Can't we all remember desperately
wanting our own versions of that pink bowling ball?)

He sees that as we get older, we accumulate more, as if it
protects us—"a passive restraint system to mortality." (I would
add that after a certain advanced age, many see "things" as the
encumbrances they are and want only time with loved ones.)

J wonders why people give up so much time earning money
to buy new things. Once we own something, it's not new. He
exempts no one from the quest for things, including himself:

"...a prisoner of my own materialistic nature, but junk has taught me to do what I can to counteract it, at least a little ... all will come to junk eventually, and much sooner than you think."

"In the junk business, we collect the ugly with the beautiful, the bizarre with the elegant, the valuable with the worthless, sometimes forget-ting which is which, or intentionally inverting them. We do it because, well, we can. We have the power. Junkers know that all of us have the authority to assign value, that we don't have to want the things we're told to want, that it's good to love that which seems to have no worth."

While cleaning my garage last summer, I came across a box with shredded paper in the corner. Just an abandoned mouse nest—we find those here in the woods. But lifting it out, who should look up at me with panicked beady eyes but a mother

field mouse, spread-ing her soft brown body over her little ones, a hopeless bravado against the monster that was me. Oh, dear. I really don't dislike mice, I just don't appreciate them in the house or garage. So I tucked her fluffy blanket back over the family and carried the box out to the woods, leaving it there with a whispered "Sorry — good luck." I figured they deserved a chance, at least.

The next day my excellent hunter Reno walked by with that distorted meow that announces his catch. *Good for you, Reno*, I thought, until I wondered — *is it her? Is it the mama who looked me in the eye? What will her babies do? Did Reno crunch the tidbits first, as she helplessly watched?* Suddenly, an ordinary scene felt like a horror movie.

Months later, I was too busy to pay much attention to the story of the cruise ship that ran aground near Italy, until I heard that my neighbor Ronda and her sister Vivian were on it! Thank goodness they were among the lucky ones in the lifeboats, but it tore at my

Do you see the white head of my totem pole's eagle watching over us all?
Every season of life has its beauty.

emotions once the connection was made. St. Thomas Island felt a lot closer when hurricanes Irma and Maria hit while my cousin Tammy was living there.

It strikes me how often we sift our news, and value things or people through the screen of our familiarity, according to how it touches us. (That's not surprising, considering how the 24/7 news cycle assaults our sensitivities by flashing traumatic events over and over!) It pleases me to see so many young people traveling or studying overseas. As they develop friendships and "those people" become "my people," we boost our chances for cooperation and survival. It's also why I'm delighted when I see young and old spending time outdoors. By tasting the freshness of clean air and water, by watching nature's babies frolic, and by embracing the rare silence that lets us hear our hearts' secret songs, we come to know the true value of the natural world. By walking in deserts, or creating our own little gardens, we come to understand the meaning of a drought. Then instead of complaining about a bit of inconvenience when it rains, we join the thirsty ground in shouting, *"Hallelujah!"*

The reality is that we *are* all as interconnected as the man, fish, and eagle on my totem pole—just carvings on the same tree of life. Though death is a natural and necessary part of the circle of life, every living thing has value, whether or not it has looked us in the eye. The more we learn to consider the costs and benefits *to all*, to think in terms of net energy expended and gained, net value or loss to the larger community and the earth, rather than just to ourselves, the more prosperity and safety we will all enjoy.

Spring
Oh, the smell of mud and moss!
The crocuses are coming!
Night is filled with a chorus of frogs
and the squawking of geese,
calling their kin from the south.
The resident beavers, freed from beneath their
glass ceiling,
reclaim the lake
and answer my playful warnings with
their own—
slap!
Painted turtles do a dance—he tickles her chin.
They come to my canoe and look
right up at me.
Are they too sleepy to be afraid,
or too much in love?
Bluebirds have already claimed house #40.
Miss Lilac prepares to unfurl her green flags,
while the pussy willows fluff up their
furry tails.
It's all so exciting!
If only there were not that ominous
something wrong.
The frightening math
of 81 degrees on the 26th of March at the
45th parallel.

    HJ

"He who sees the light in everything and everyone is enlightened."

A colleague wrote at the bottom of his emails, "He who sees the light in everything and everyone is enlightened." To see the light, the good, the potential in *everything* allows us to embrace the imperfect, to pass things up, to pass things on, knowing we'll find more light around the next bend. To see the light in *everyone* brings joy and learning and compassion to the one looking and empowers the other to shine even more brightly.

When I asked my colleague where he got that quote, he said he thinks he saw it on a teabag. What could be trashier than a used teabag? Yet to the open and humble soul, even this bit of garbage might hold freedom at the end of a little brown string.

Sometimes it takes darkness to see a special light.

Appendix A

The List: Shades of Green

There are plenty of lists out there, in books, pamphlets, magazines, and the internet. Here's another, one to make your own, or use in your favorite discussion group. Not everyone can do everything, but we can each do something. Pick the ones that are feasible for you, that sound fun to you, that excite you. Check off whether you could, will, or already do that thing. Then add your own ideas. Do a little or a lot. Take the list out periodically and see how far you've come, how far you might want to go. And always count your blessings.

SHADES OF GREEN	I CAN	I WILL	I DO
Appreciate a smaller home dwelling (house/apartment/tent/cave)			
Consider heating and cooling needs when deciding home needs			
Use salvaged or recycled materials when building, finishing, expanding, or renovating			
Use space efficiently			
Use or mix paints, cleaners, materials from recycling centers			
Check for electronics first at the recycling center			
Shop at thrift stores, rummage sales, or the "Curbside Boutique" for clothing, household goods, furniture, gifts, and knickknacks			

SHADES OF GREEN	I CAN	I WILL	I DO
Minimize energy usage Have an energy audit			
Have efficient windows or glass			
Have efficient insulation			
Use a clean-burning wood stove			
Lower the thermostat in winter			
Raise the thermostat in summer (if you have air conditioning)			
Warm or cool only the rooms needed at the time			
Use fans instead of air-conditioning			
Find a shady spot outside			
Wear warm clothes in winter and cool ones in summer			
Replace old appliances with energy-efficient models			
Turn off lights and electronics			
Use halogen incandescent, compact fluorescent, or LED bulbs			
Cool with open windows and shade trees			
Purchase as much wind-power as possible			
Dry clothes on the line			
Minimize oil and gasoline use Avoid plastics, in both products and packaging			
Keep tires properly inflated and engine tuned			
Drive a fuel-efficient, hybrid, or electric car			
Use public transportation			
Bike or walk whenever possible			
Combine trips			
Carpool			
Avoid rush-hour idling			
Turn off the engine			

SHADES OF GREEN	I CAN	I WILL	I DO
Minimize waste Disassemble and recycle what you can			
Reuse cloth or other bags for groceries and other purchases			
Avoid packaging in food and goods			
Recycle cans, plastics, glass, and paper			
Donate anything you no longer need to someone who does			
Compost			
Act politically Check candidate records on environmental issues before voting			
Contribute to environmental research and advocacy			
Stand up for the air, land, wildlife, and water in local and global matters			
Invite speakers to educate neighborhoods and schools on sustainability			
Create your own style; refuse pressure from advertising and peers			
Accept and embrace your hair color; skip the expensive, smelly, toxic chemicals			
Find a low-maintenance hairstyle			
Accept and embrace diversity in your lawn; skip the expensive, smelly, toxic chemicals			
Accept natural nails; skip the expensive, smelly, toxic chemicals			
Consider /try natural, cruelty-free cosmetics			
Use natural or homemade cleaners and skip the expensive, smelly, toxic chemicals			
Maintain a small lawn (or none)			
Plant natives			
Plant trees			
Fight aliens like buckthorn (preferably by mechanical means, skipping the expensive, smelly, toxic chemicals)			

SHADES OF GREEN	I CAN	I WILL	I DO
Use a quiet reel lawn mower and use the noisy, smelly one only for long grass or mulching			
Use an electric mower or mulcher			
Share tools with neighbors			
Wait for things to come to you, rather than rush out and buy them			
Read a book instead of watching TV (unless it's a great show)			
Avoid commercials and ads or talk back to them			
Opt for a game at home rather than going to a movie (unless it's a great movie)			
Wait for the great movie to come out on DVD			
Check out library books, CDs, DVDs instead of buying them			
Share (not pirate!) books, CDs, and DVDs with friends			
Pay up front and skip paying interest whenever possible			
Consciously reject over-consumption in favor of a more humble, realistic, practical, sustainable and, yes, joyful lifestyle of striving for only what you truly want and need			
Reject perfectionism			
Appreciate the wabi sabi grace of simplicity and well-used things			
Be unashamed and unapologetic about buying used goods or rescuing from the trash. Share your good fortune			
Teach kids about recycling through art projects			
Promote environmental education			
STOP to watch the stunning swans, listen to the loons, breathe in the smells of soil, float with the turtles, rest your body and fill your soul, and feel joyful in your resolve to live lightly on the earth. Live contentedly in keeping with your values			
Add your own ideas—and share them with me! holly@hollyonthelake.com			

Appendix B

Helpers for
Changing Habits

If you want to change your spending habits, I suggest examining them first. Make a list of ways you spend your own or your family's money. This will be easier and more complete if you take a look at your automatic withdrawals, credit card statements, and checkbook records, but don't forget the cash. Jot it down every time a bit dribbles out of that hole in your pocket. After gathering your data for a month, sit down with the list and ask yourself two questions about each item:

How important is this item or activity to me?
What are my options or alternatives?

After doing this a few times, you will automatically ask yourself these questions *before* a purchase. Instead of feeling pressured or restricted, you will begin to feel empowered. Of course there are areas where choices are limited, but once you start asking the questions, more choices become visible.

You might want to try the same methods to see how you are spending your time. Keep track for a while, then ask yourself the same two questions.

Appendix C

Keys to Carry
While Shopping, Cruising for Junk, or Decluttering

The media and our own minds bombard us with mantras that make us want to acquire and hold onto things. Keep these questions handy as an antidote when you're bitten by the buy bug, or when you're having trouble letting go of things. Laminate your favorite and put it on your key ring or tape it to your wallet. You'll be surprised at how much easier it becomes when we take back our minds from the media.

The colorful clothes at the state fair always tempt me, so I have to remind myself that my closet is full!

KEYS TO CARRY

What might be influencing my desire for this? Is it real, or illusion?

Is this beautiful? Useful? Flattering? Or just fashionable or a fad?

Is this congruent with my values? Is it really me?

How often in the last year have I needed this? How often will I need it?

Does someone else need or want this more than I do?

Am I sure I don't already have one, or more than one?

Do I need to own it, or could I borrow, rent, or make one?

Could I use something else?

Do I want/need this more than the money/time/power I'm trading for it?

If I buy this:

> Will it be a joy or a burden? For how long?

> Where will I store it?

> Who profits? Is it a fair price?

> What will I do with it when I no longer need or want it?

> How does its production and disposal affect the earth?

> How does it affect the seventh generation?

Appendix D
Mantras to Combat Media and Peer Pressure

I'm not cheap, I'm frugal, thrifty, green, and wise.
I like wabi sabi, the art of imperfection.
I can think, I can wait, I can fast.

You've read how these mantras have influenced my life. Of course you can adopt them, or you can adapt them or create your own. Here are some ideas. Highlight the ones that you like. Put your favorites on brightly colored slips in your checkbook, on a Post-it Note on your credit card, or on your key chain. Make up your own. Set it to a melody and sing it.

I don't really love it.	I don't really need it.
It's not that important to me.	It's not my priority.
I already have one.	I don't need another.
Mine is good enough.	Mine is clean enough.
I'd rather have sanity than sanitary.	Too sanitary is dead.
Nothing's perfect.	Nobody's perfect.
I'll wait and find a better one.	Who cares what they think?
I'd rather be unique than trendy.	I'd rather be creative.
I'd rather be artsy.	I'd rather be green.
I'd rather be earthy.	I'd rather be me.
I'd rather have the money.	I'd rather have the time.

Appendix E
How We Renovated My Totem Pole

What a labor of love, and I love my neighbors for all their help. Ronda and Rachel helped me get it out of the car on April 18, 2009. Bill brought his guest and two wooden dollies over to move the heavy rain-soaked pole into the garage for drying—when I wasn't even home! Many people gave me ideas and advice. Then the steps began:

1) Use wood hardener to solidify what I could.
2) Remove the wood that had rotted into dust.
3) Cut off the bottom eight inches and spray for ants , saying "I'm sorry" as I kill the critters, yes, with smelly chemicals.
4) With John's help, "bandage" the eagle with tape.
5) With John's help, bit by bit, fill the large cavity with polyether foam, made by mixing liquids A and B, a cup at a time, and pouring it in as it expanded.
6) Create a new beak by pouring the foam into my plastic-covered hand held up to the head, and holding it there until it hardened.
7) Carve the beak and head from the hardened foam.
8) Cover the renewed head parts and beak with a thin layer of Bondo.
9) Smooth the Bondo with a rasp, but not too much. It has to be rustic, like the wood.
10) Paint the Bondo, then dry-brush to make it look old and match the original wood parts.
11) Sand the most weathered wing and use paint and stain to make the two wings match.

12) With John's amazing ingenuity and reassurance that we weren't killing my eagle, drill and insert a steel rod through both wings and the body, tightening them down with bolts on both ends.

13) Secure wings with shims and Bondo.

14) Amazingly, find two perfect eagle eyes looking up at me from my workbench downstairs (salvaged from an old plastic owl that lost its feathers and bit the dust).

15) Paint the background for the eyes and glue them on.

16) Fill the major cracks with wood putty.

17) Sand shoulders, knees, and other end-grain areas.

18) Rub wood putty into end-grain areas and resand.

19) Use paint and heart-redwood stain to renew a deep-brown color to the grayed wood and add protection.

20) Rebuild the rotted-off sides of base with poly foam.

21) Cover new foam parts of base with Bondo, creating vertical grooves with putty knife.

22) Paint new base areas with dark-brown paint.

23) Fill vertical grooves with wood putty.

24) Stain base with heart-redwood stain.

25) With Jeff, Rachel, Rick, and Shari's help, move totem pole to deck and place on new base.

26) Bill generously made and fitted a wood brace to rest eagle against house.

27) Stain the brace.

28) John brought six-inch wood screws and idea for bolting eagle to house through brace.

29) Bill brought ten-inch wood screws and helped screw eagle to house through brace, pole to new base, and base to deck. (This totem pole is not going anywhere!)

30) Bill brought "Moonglow" solar lights to softly light the totem pole in its new home.

We didn't have a potlatch when we raised it, but on November 22, I had the neighbors over for a "feast" to thank them. I shared some of the fascinating lore I'd learned during my totem pole summer as we celebrated the addition to the neighborhood.

Many of my neighbors helped, but John was his primary physician.

Days darken,

time to
curl up and read

Suggested Reading

Here are a few of my favorites, but ask a librarian or check the catalog for subjects such as sustainable living, green movement, thriftiness, environmental protection, and environmentalism to find hundreds of titles.

Clark, Dawson, and Bredehoft. *How Much Is Enough?: Everything You Need to Know to Steer Clear of Overindulgence and Raise Likable, Responsible, and Respectful Children*, Marlowe & Company, 2004

Common Ground Media. *Dirt! The Movie*, DVD, 2010

Crawford, Matthew. *Shop Class as Soulcraft: An Inquiry into the Value of Work*, Penguin Press, 2009. Published in London as *The Case For Working With Your Hands*; Viking, 2009

Eighner, Lars. "On Dumpster Diving" in *Pushcart Book of Essays*, 1992

Goleman, Daniel. *Ecological Intelligence: the Hidden Impacts of What We Buy*, New York: Broadway, 2010

Hodge, Oliver. Sundance Channel. *Garbage Warrior*. Award-winning film about Michael Reynolds and his fight to build off-the-grid self-sufficient communities, DVD, 2007

Jarvis, Cheryl. *The Necklace: Thirteen Women and the Experiment That Transformed Their Lives*, New York: Ballantine, 2008

Pritchett, Laura, ed. *Going Green: True Tales from Gleaners, Scavengers, and Dumpster Divers*, University of Oklahoma Press, 2009, (includes the essay "Blacktop Cuisine" by Michael Engelhard)

Roberts, James A. *Shiny Objects: Why We Spend Money We Don't Have in Search of Happiness Money Can't Buy.* Harper One, 2011

Sandbeck, Ellen. *Green Barbarians,* New York: Simon and Schuster, 2010

Treuer, Anton. *Everything You Wanted to Know About Indians But Were Afraid to Ask,* St. Paul, MN: Borealis Books, 2012

Walsh, David Allen. *No: Why Kids—of All Ages—need to Hear It and Ways Parents Can Say It,* New York: Free, 2007

For Children and Adults

Janisch, Heinz, & Leffler, Silke. *I Have a Little Problem, Said the Bear,* New York, NorthSouth, 2009

McDonnell, Patrick. *The Gift of Nothing,* New York: Little, Brown, 2005

Menchin, Scott. *Taking a Bath with the Dog and Other Things That Make Me Happy,* Cambridge, MA: Candlewick, 2007

Ross, Tony. *Centipede's 100 Shoes,* New York: H. Holt, 2003

Smith, David J. *If the World Were a Village: A Book about the World's People,* Toronto: Kids Can Press, 2nd edition, 2011

Taback, Simms. *Joseph Had a Little Overcoat,* New York: Scholastic, 2000

Wong, Janet S., and David Roberts. *The Dumpster Diver,* Cambridge, MA: Candlewick, 2007

Wood, Douglas. *Grandad's Prayers of the Earth*, Paw Prints, 2009

Having been a librarian, I don't *buy* many books, but I must have my nature guides on hand. This beaver lived outside my window one winter and popped up when the warm spells let him. I read and watched amazing documentaries about their building skill and strong family ties.

Acknowledgments

Several times as I wrote this book, I thought, *This is the hardest chapter.* But *this* — trying to adequately thank all the people who had a role in bringing me to this place — is impossible. This book would never have happened without all the wonderful "characters" in it and supporting me!

Mom and Dad (Audrey and Bud Jorgensen) are at the core of everything, having taught me so well what is important in life. I've learned from my brother, James, and sister, Nancy, much more than they realize. My nieces, Angela, Kym, and Amy; nephew, Jeremiah; and grand-nephew, Benjamin, with their sweet, courageous hearts, give me hope for this changing world.

Gary Gilson, Marti Erickson, and Doug Wallace have kept me going with their advice and cheers for decades. Editors Nick Tramdack, John Toren, and Marly Cornell kept my thoughts and words on track — not an easy task with this highly distractible writer! Pat Morris has generously blessed me with her extensive experience and sound advice for years. Designer Paul Nylander patiently tried every idea I suggested and used his considerable expertise to weave my pictures and text into a real book.

I gratefully learned from each of my brilliant advisors, but the fact that they didn't always agree taught me that *I had* to be the ultimate boss of my book. So if you don't like my punctuation or style, it's on me, not them. I often chose to listen to my voice more than the rules.

I've had so much help and encouragement on so many projects. Each endeavor, successful or not, has been a building block in the wonderful life that I am blessed to write about. Below are just a few who were especially helpful as I honed my too-voluminous thoughts into this book. I apologize to the *many* not named and I thank you all more than I can say.

Carol J. Anderson, Ph.D., Connie Anderson, Kim Battern, Hollis Booker, Judge Tanya Bransford, Susan and Steve Buck, Kim Colbert, Jake Coldren, Maxine Coldren, Peggy Drews, Scott Edelstein, Cynthia Edmon, Bernie and Mike Farrell, Chris Farrell, Dale Faulstich, Julia Fox, Carol and Mike Gillen, Lois Greiman, Julie Gunderson, Dawne Jourdain, Debbie Kalish, Amy Kennedy-Fosseen, B.B. King, Dr. Bill Kueppers, Rubin Latz, The Loft Literary Center, Sue and Eric Lund, Taj Mahal, Dorie McClelland, Roger Michalski, Midwest Independent Publishing Association, Michael Monroe, Stephanie Morris, Debra Mueller, Angela Norell, Bruce Peck, Linda Pinnell, Mary Roon, Ellen Sandbeck, Pat Schoenecker, Don Shelby, Maryl Skinner, Shirley Spanhanks, Brenda Starr, Norton Stillman, Koko Taylor, Dr. Anton Treuer, Dick Waterman, George Winston, Women of Words

About the Author

Photo by Carol Gillen

Holly Jorgensen has been a teacher, librarian, performer, and writer, among other adventures. She speaks often on themes such as "Saving Money, the Planet, and Your Sanity," "Connecting with Mother Nature's Other Children," and "Strong Girls (or Kids) for a Green World." Her newest passion is sharing her love of nature through her photography and words. Articles by and about Holly have appeared in the Minneapolis Star Tribune, the Minnesota Women's Press, the Minnesota Sun Current, the Hutchinson Leader, and WINK: Writers in the Know, and she has appeared on Twin Cities Public Television and Minnesota Public Radio. She lives happily among critters just outside of Minneapolis. To book her; read her blog; purchase books, cards, and framed photos; or find out more about Northern Holly Creations, please visit www.hollyonthelake.com